# Shetland for Bairns

## by David Cockayne & friends

Shetland For Bairns

First published by The Shetland Times Ltd, 2020

ISBN 978-1-910997-31-4

Copyright © Jane Cockayne, 2020

All rights reserved

No part of this publication may be reproduced, stored in a retrieval system, or transmitted, in any form, by any means, electronic, mechanical, photocopying, recording or otherwise, without the prior written permission of the publishers.

British Library Cataloguing-in-Publication Data.

A catalogue record for this book is available from the British Library.

Printed and published by The Shetland Times Ltd., Gremista, Lerwick, Shetland, Scotland ZE1 0PX.

# Foreword

I first had the pleasure of working with Jane Cockayne during my time as editor at *Shetland Life* magazine. Jane created an excellent children's story called 'The Magic Toolbox' that featured in the magazine. It was during this time that she told me about this project – to develop a book for bairns, by bairns. Started at the kitchen table by herself and son David, the aim of the book was to be inclusive as possible, and involve as many bairns as possible. Driven by Jane and David's enthusiasm, the result of this ambitious project is this fantastic guide to Shetland for bairns.

I was really excited when Jane asked if my children, Hansi and Lena, would be interested in doing part of the history for the book. The bairns were over-the-moon to get a trip to Mousa and a picnic at Staneydale, and I was certainly up for it – a chance to geek out on history, what wasn't to like? I love Shetland's rich history which spans back many thousands of years. Showing children places like Mousa and Jarlshof brings history to life in a way that can never be replicated in a classroom. This book is perfect for getting out of the classroom and getting your hands and feet guttery as you learn.

This book is the perfect companion to the summer holidays and should always be enjoyed with a good dash of fun!

So, for David, and all the other young explorers out there, here is a favourite quote of mine from Peter Pan creator, J. M. Barrie: "Young boys [and girls!] should never be sent to bed. They always wake up a day older, and then before you know it, they're grown."

*Laurie Goodlad*
*(Curator of Scalloway Museum)*

# Acknowledgements

*I wanted to make a book about Shetland because there are so many fun things to do and places to visit. One of my favourite places to go is the rope swing at Kergord. When I was making the book I met lots of people who taught me new facts about Shetland and shared their ideas of fun places to go for adventures, thank you.*

David Cockayne (Age 10)

Shetland For Bairns started at the kitchen table when David began to make a scrapbook about his adventures around Shetland. Over time David wondered if we could make a "real book" so we approached Charlotte Black at The Shetland Times who asked us to make a mock up page and David chose to research Shetland's woodlands as he loves exploring them. We asked our friend, Phil Laver, if he could help us with ideas for page layouts, as he is a fantastic graphic designer. Phil gave David lots of good tips and did a brilliant job translating David's mock up page onto the computer. We will always be very thankful for Phil's guidance and support at the outset of this project. Charlotte Black gave David a contract in December 2018 and from then we have been researching many aspects of life in Shetland. We are thankful to Charlotte for believing in the project and for being brave enough to give an eight year old a book contract!

It was a funny feeling handing over the manuscript (which looked like a giant scrapbook) to the Shetland Times after working on it for 18 months. We are full of admiration for designer Steven Cheverton for his ability to keep faithful to the original manuscript whilst enhancing it at the same time! You have worked so hard and produced a visual treat for bairns which is both informative and most of all fun!

It became apparent that if the book was truly going to be Shetland For Bairns then we needed to talk to children from all over Shetland and hear their ideas. It is true to say that we could not have made this book without all the bairns and families that have been involved. Children have contributed in all sorts of ways, some have researched entire topics, while others have contributed a drawing or a photo of themselves doing an activity they enjoy. We have learned so much as we have listened to what other families get up to on their Shetland adventures and discovered places we did not know existed! As you read the book you will see the names of the children that have contributed to the various sections and a full acknowledgment of those who have contributed photos and illustrations can be found at the back of the book.

We are indebted to all the parents, carers, teachers and professionals who have supported their bairns to make their contributions.

We are hugely grateful to the staff at Shetland Amenity Trust for their support and could not have made the book without their knowledge, expertise and enthusiasm. In particular we want to thank Jenny Murray who showed David around the museum store, which is like an Aladdin's cave full of Shetland's treasures! Brian Smith was very generous with his time and made some valuable observations and suggestions as he read through the history section. We can't thank Ian Tait enough for his enthusiasm and ability to see the project through the eyes of a bairn! After reading an initial draft of the book Ian made helpful and fun suggestions, which have added a more interesting angle to the books presentation and content. David also enjoyed going to visit Rory Tallack who is Shetland's Geopark Manager. He explained to us what it means for Shetland to be a Geopark and has contributed a fantastic page with the help of his bairns, Thea and Malin. We would also like to thank Sandy Middleton and Val Turner for their helpfulness in providing information and photos.

It is true to say that we could not have made the book without Laurie Goodlad. From the outset she has been enthusiastic and has offered to help in any way she can. Laurie has proof read much of the history section and checked that we have got our facts right! She also researched the Ancient History section with her bairns Hansi and Lena. Laurie has been incredibly generous in allowing us to use many of her photos and along with the Shetland Life magazine she promoted our project, which greatly helped our research.

We would like to thank the schools that have helped us investigate topics for the book. Helen Robertson at Hamnavoe School was very helpful and it was fun to visit and meet Miss Mikolajczak's class. We would also like to thank David's class and their P4 teachers, Joanna Manson and Dawn Mainland who researched the Stewart Earls and the Scalloway Castle. Thanks is also due to Hannah Irvine and the pupils of the North Roe School and to Darcy Cook and the staff of the Fetlar School for their creativity and enthusiasm.

We would like to thank the staff of the Tangwick Haa and the Quendale Mill for all their support and for taking the time to meet the bairns that visited in their quest for historical information. The staff at the Scalloway Museum have been so encouraging and helpful and we would like to particularly acknowledge Billy Moore, who welcomed David's class on their castle visit. Billy also opened up the museum especially to allow David to photograph various artefacts.

The Shetland Recreational Trust and the Active Schools team were really good at highlighting the range of sporting opportunities there are for bairns in Shetland. Stephanie Bain at Ability Shetland and Donna Murray from Sports for All were more than helpful and made invaluable contributions to various sections of the book. Terry and Grace at The Cornerstone Cafe in Scalloway opened their doors for a drop in session to gather ideas from families in Shetland – thank you for providing such a welcoming place to do our research. Short Breaks for Children took on the play park challenge and reviewed three parks for the book – thank you for the time you took to do this! We also want to thank Jan and Pete Bevington at the Hillswick Wildlife Sanctuary for their contribution and to Johanna David for allowing us to photograph the special wedding dress at the Tangwick Haa. Karen MacKelvie from RSPB Shetland was wildly enthusiastic about promoting opportunities for children to engage with nature in Shetland, thank you so much for all the information you provided! As you read through the book you will see that there are many groups, such as the Swan Trust, Scouts and sports clubs, who have contributed a photograph and sometimes brief descriptions of what they get up to – we know folks are busy so we really appreciate all those who have taken the time to do this. Particular thanks goes to Cathy Mann, Jenny Teale, Martin Summers, Cyndi Pottinger, Rachel Williamson and Carrie MacDonald.

During our research journey we have got to know some talented artists and we have been humbled by their enthusiasm and generosity towards the book project. We would like to thank Hugh Harrop who has allowed us to feature many of his wonderful wildlife photographs and has given us expert advice on Shetland's cool creatures, he has done everything he can to be helpful. We are blessed to have got to know Gilly Bridle over these past few months as she worked on an exquisite paper cut for the dialect section, when we saw the paper cut process we were in awe! Gilly is a hugely talented and kind lady. Bryan Mouat has cleverly brought to life some of Shetland's curious characters in his fun and brilliant illustrations as well as creating a spot the difference feature, we want to thank him for the time and thought he put into doing this – you are a genius! We would also like to thank Maria Barclay for allowing us to feature her beautiful song about the Peerie Lavericks and Ann Marie and Margaret Anderson for allowing us to share their brilliant bairns books. We also want to thank Valerine Watt for allowing us to mention her books and Itchy Coo publications for giving us their blessing to highlight the brilliant work they do to keep local dialects alive! We have had fun with Alex Purbrick and her family and love their enthusiasm for outdoor adventures, thank you Alex for your contribution to the "arts and crafts with natural materials" section and for going on a photo shoot up north!

Terri Malcolmson, Janette Budge, Hazel Tindall, Wendy Inkster and Tracey Hawkins have been really kind in contributing to a knitting feature, which we hope inspires bairns to try their hand at makkin. We would also like to thank Garry at the Sandness Mill for allowing us to use some of their photographs and the Peerie Makkers for their fantastic feedback. Jonathan and Chloe Kerr have provided beautiful family photos and have given a lot of time towards helping with many sections of the book, especially Aboot da Banks. We would also like to thank Kathryn Spence, Graeme Howell and Esther Renwick at Shetland Arts for their input and helpfulness in the book project. We really appreciate the time it took Chloe Tallack to put together a piece about what the Shetland Library offers bairns and also want to thank Raman Mundair for her helpful suggestions about celebrating Shetland's diverse communities, which has became a special part of making this book.

David's grandparents, aunties, uncles and cousins have all been very encouraging and enthusiastic during the book making process. We would like to thank dad in particular for his photo contributions and book making knowledge!

We acknowledge that this book only scratches the surface of what is available in Shetland for bairns. We have tried our best to include as much as possible but know that there will be many things that we have missed. We have left space at the end of the book for you to feature your very own Shetland facts and adventures. As a way of saying a heartfelt thank you to all who have made contributions to this book we are donating 50% of the royalties towards fun and interactive learning experiences for bairns, which will be planned and delivered in partnership with the Shetland Amenity Trust.

Finally, we want to say a huge thank you to Anna who has been incredibly patient as we have spent many hours on adventures, at meetings and typing at the kitchen table. We also want to express our gratitude to our IT advisor, Tom, who has given us much needed technical advice and support throughout the project – we could not have done it without you!

We hope that you enjoy this book and that it inspires you to be curious and adventurous in Shetland.

*Jane, David's Mum*

# Contents

A Shetland Map .................................. 8

Introduction ....................................... 9

Ancient History ................................ 10

Old Scatness Broch and
  Iron Age Village ............................. 11

The Vikings / Stewart Earls ......... 12

Houses and Homes ........................ 13

Crofts Today .................................... 14

The Shetland Bus ........................... 15

St Ninians Treasure ....................... 16

Past and Present ............................ 17

Curious Characters ....................... 18

School ............................................... 20

Fishing and the Sea ...................... 21

Transport ......................................... 22

Coming and Going ....................... 23

Dialect .............................................. 24

Folklore ............................................ 26

Arts and Entertainment ............... 28

Museums ......................................... 30

Peerie Lavericks song ................. 31

Festivals, Shows & Celebrations ... 32

Knitting ............................................ 33

Scones and Bannocks .................. 34

Cari's Paet Story ............................ 35

Fun Places Outside ...................... 36

Beaches ............................................ 37

Aboot da Banks ............................. 38

Woodlands ...................................... 39

Arts and Crafts with
  Natural Materials ........................ 40

Cool Creatures ............................... 41

Geopark ........................................... 42

Looking after our Environment .... 43

Parks and Community Gardens ... 44

Camping and Caravanning ........ 46

Leisure Centres ............................. 47

Sport .................................................. 48

Groups and Clubs ......................... 49

The Magic Toolbox ....................... 50

Your Own Shetland Adventures! ... 51

Quiz ................................................... 52

Bibliography/References ............ 53

Photo Credits ................................. 54

# A map of Shetland

**This book is for all my friends and to Ms Willis who I absolutely loved being my teacher.**

**If you have got a dream just go for it!**

# Introduction

Shetland is a special place to live or visit. In this book children from around Shetland have shared their favourite places to go as well as fun activity ideas. Here are some interesting facts about Shetland...

Around 23,000 people live on Shetland.

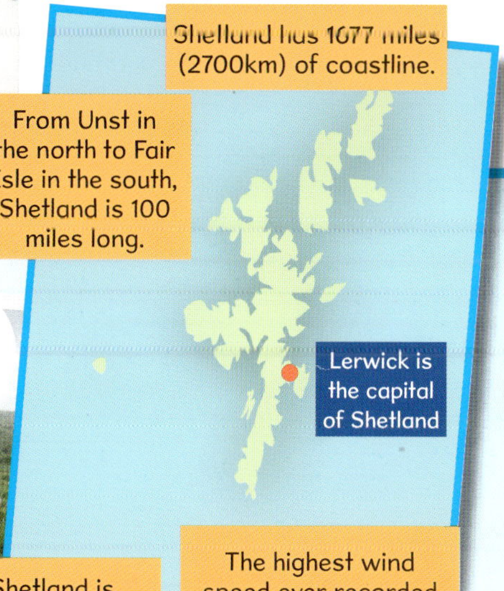

Shetland has 1677 miles (2700km) of coastline.

From Unst in the north to Fair Isle in the south, Shetland is 100 miles long.

Lerwick is the capital of Shetland.

The Shetland flag uses the colours of the Scottish flag with a Scandinavian style cross.
The design of the flag tells an interesting story and celebrates an important part of Shetland's history:

- In 1195 (during part of the period of the Vikings/Norse settlers), Shetland became part of Norway.
- In 1469 Princess Margaret of Denmark was promised in marriage to King James III of Scotland. By this time Shetland was owned by Denmark who needed to give a dowry (money or property given by the bride's family to her future husband) to King James III. The King of Denmark did not have enough money so he gave Shetland to Scotland with the understanding he could get Shetland back when he could pay up.
- Shetland has never been redeemed by Denmark and has remained part of Scotland since 1469.

The Shetland Museum and Archives look after 18,000–20,000 fascinating historical artefacts.

The 60° North line of latitude passes through Shetland.

Shetland is made up of over 100 islands with people staying on 16 of them. The biggest island is called **"The Mainland"**.

The highest wind speed ever recorded on Shetland was 73 knots (89mph) at Muckle Flugga lighthouse on 1st January, 1992. There were unofficial record gusts of over 150 knots (173mph).

The highest point on Shetland is the top of Ronas Hill which is 450 metres (1476ft).

**Mavis Grind** is the narrowest piece of land on Shetland's Mainland. At its narrowest point it is only 33 metres wide. It is said to be the only place in the UK where you can throw a stone from the Atlantic Ocean overland into the North Sea (if you are strong!)

Shetland is 110 miles north of the Scottish Mainland.

Shetland has one of the biggest oil and gas terminals in Europe at Sullom Voe.

For every person in Shetland there are more than ten sheep!

It is 600 miles (965km) from Lerwick, the capital of Shetland, to London.

The most northerly bus shelter in the UK is at Baltasound in Unst. It is a fun place to visit as it is regularly redecorated.

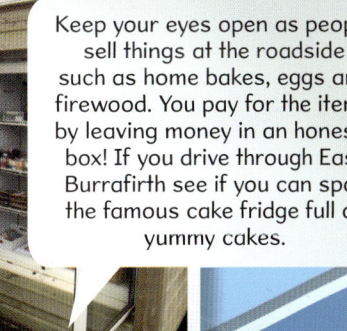

Keep your eyes open as people sell things at the roadside such as home bakes, eggs and firewood. You pay for the items by leaving money in an honesty box! If you drive through East Burrafirth see if you can spot the famous cake fridge full of yummy cakes.

There are 12 tammie norries (puffins) in Unst – how many can you find?

On a clear night during the winter you can see the Mirrie Dancers (Northern Lights).

It is 10,230 miles (16463.589km) from Lerwick to Sydney, Australia.

# Ancient History

Shetland's ancient history was researched by Hansi and Lena Pottinger, with a little help from their mum Laurie.

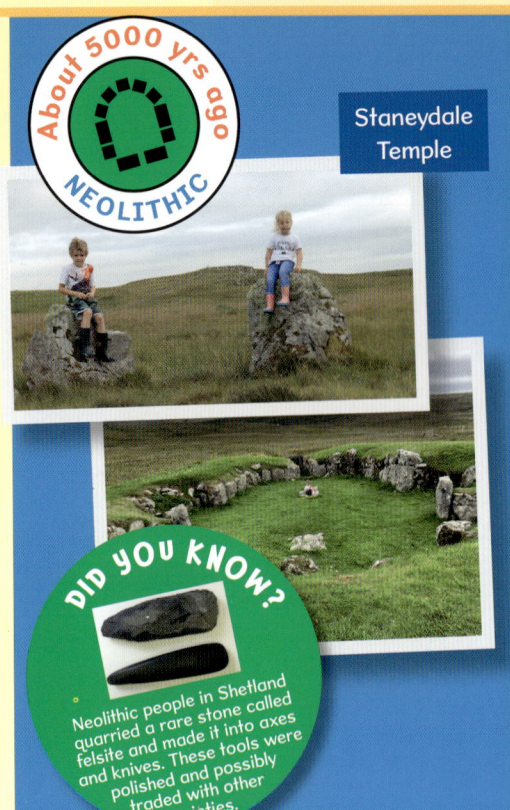

*About 5000 yrs ago — NEOLITHIC*

Staneydale Temple

**DID YOU KNOW?** Neolithic people in Shetland quarried a rare stone called felsite and made it into axes and knives. These tools were polished and possibly traded with other societies.

*3-4000 yrs ago — BRONZE AGE*

Jarlshof

*2000 yrs ago — IRON AGE*

Storm Petrel

Mousa Broch

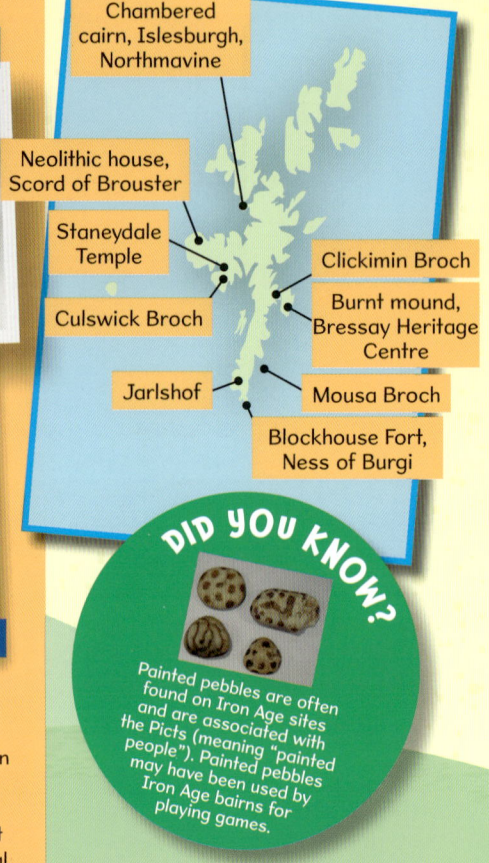

Chambered cairn, Islesburgh, Northmavine
Neolithic house, Scord of Brouster
Staneydale Temple
Culswick Broch
Jarlshof
Clickimin Broch
Burnt mound, Bressay Heritage Centre
Mousa Broch
Blockhouse Fort, Ness of Burgi

**DID YOU KNOW?** Painted pebbles are often found on Iron Age sites and are associated with the Picts (meaning "painted people"). Painted pebbles may have been used by Iron Age bairns for playing games.

About 5000 years ago Shetland's first settlers arrived and built homes and farmed the land for the first time. If you look at Shetland's landscape you can see evidence of the structures that these first settlers built such as the remains of cairns and small houses. The first settlers kept sheep and cattle and there is also evidence that shows the field systems they used to work the land.

We explored Staneydale Temple on the west mainland of Shetland. As you approach the temple there are two standing stones that lead to the door. When you are at Staneydale Temple you will notice that if you look around you can't see the sea from any direction. It is not known what the building was used for but it was called a temple because it has similarities to other temples in Malta. It is the largest Neolithic building in Shetland.

The Bronze Age was a short period in Shetland and the most noticeable structures you can see from this time are burnt mounds. Archaeologists still don't know what they were used for. In folklore they are called "fairy knowes" or "trowie hills". Archaeologists have lots of ideas of why burnt mounds were made including places for tanning hides, brewing beer or for using as saunas!

In order to make bronze you need two raw materials: copper and tin. Copper is found in Shetland and the nearest tin is found in Cornwall!

Jarlshof is a fantastic site as it covers every period of settlement in Shetland from the first settlers 5000 years ago to the rule of Earl Patrick Stewart around 1600. While we were there we visited the Bronze Age smithy. Evidence suggests that there might have been a skilled metalsmith that worked there. A bronze pin was found at Jarlshof and it is identical to one found in excavations in Ireland.

One of the greatest legacies left by Shetland's mysterious Iron Age people are the brochs. The only place in the world that brochs are found is in the north and west of Scotland. The brochs are about 2000 years old and there are about 120 broch sites in Shetland. Archaeologists still don't know what brochs were used for and their actual purpose is still a mystery!

We visited Mousa broch, which is the best preserved broch in the world. It stands 13 metres high and is now the summer home to a breeding colony of seabirds called storm petrels (alamooties in Shetland). The birds are tiny and fly into the broch late in the evening to avoid being caught by predators such as rats and hedgehogs.

Over time people have taken stones from the brochs to make new buildings. At one time there was a broch on the Mainland, opposite the isle of Mousa. It is thought that it might have been identical to Mousa broch. It collapsed long ago and most of the stones were used to build another township nearby that now also stands in ruins.

**Tick if you made it!**

- STANEYDALE TEMPLE
- JARLSHOF
- MOUSA BROCH
- SCORD OF BROUSTER
- A BURNT MOUND
- CLICKIMIN BROCH
- CHAMBERED CAIRN, ISLESBURGH
- OTHER
- CULSWICK BROCH
- OTHER
- OTHER
- NESS OF BURGI

## World Wide Timeline

 Great Pyramid built 4500 years ago

 Stonehenge completed 3500 years ago

 Foundations of Rome laid 2800 years ago

 Great Wall of China begun 2200 years ago

# Old Scatness Broch & Iron Age Village

Old Scatness is an archaeological site which has Viking, Iron Age, Pictish and Mediaeval remains. The site was hidden underground until it was discovered in 1975 when a road was being built through what was thought to be a natural mound. Since then Scatness has been extensively excavated and each year archaeologists make new discoveries. During the summer months the site is open for visitors and you can join a guided tour, visit the shop and dress up and play ancient games.

An aerial photograph of the **Scatness** site, can you spot the shapes and remains of the ancient buildings?

**Chris Dyer** is an archaeologist who knows a lot about the Scatness site and he likes to share interesting facts with visitors.

## Spot the Difference

During the summer you can visit Scatness Broch and Iron Age village and dress up in clothes from long ago!
Can you spot six differences between these photos?

Old Scatness Broch and Iron age Village

### DID YOU KNOW?

A Pictish carving of a bear was found on a stone in one of the ancient buildings at Scatness. It is an interesting find because as far as we know bears have never lived in Shetland! See if you can find this special stone in the Shetland Museum, Lerwick.

### Tick if you made it!

Old Scatness Broch and Iron age Village ◯

Shetland Amenity Trust: Telephone 01595 694688    Website: www.shetlandamenity.org

# The Vikings (Norse settlers)

The Vikings were researched by Seth Corbett

A Viking oven at Jarlshof

At Catound quarry you can see where Vikings carved into the rocks

Viking longship and house replicas, Unst

Girlsta Loch

Vikings or Norse settlers sailed to Shetland on longships around 800 AD, which is about 1200 years ago. Some of my favourite Viking facts are:

**CATPUND QUARRY, CUNNINGSBURGH.**
At this quarry you can still see where the Vikings cut blocks out of the soapstone rock to make bowls.

**VIKING OVEN, JARLSHOF.**
At Jarlshof you can see the remains of many Viking longhouses. The Vikings even put ovens for cooking in their homes!

**VIKING LONGHOUSE AND SHIP RECONSTRUCTION, UNST.**
Unst is a great place to visit to discover more about Shetland's Viking past. The remains of at least 60 longhouses have been found as well as artefacts such as a beautifully made soapstone lamp! You can visit the replica Viking longship and longhouse, they help you imagine how the Vikings sailed from Norway to Shetland and what their homes were like when they lived here.

**VIKING PRINCESS, LOCH OF GIRLSTA.**
Legend tells us that a Viking chief and explorer called Floki of The Ravens sailed to Shetland around 800 AD (about 1200 years ago). It is said that he kept ravens on his boat as they helped him find land. His daughter, Princess Gerhildr, is thought to have drowned in the Loch of Girlsta. The loch was named after her and it is said that she was buried on the island in the middle of the loch.

**DID YOU KNOW?** 
Welcome to VEENSGARTH
Víkings-garðr
(Old Norse: Viking's Farm)
About 95% of Shetland's place names come from old Norse language.

# Stewart Earls

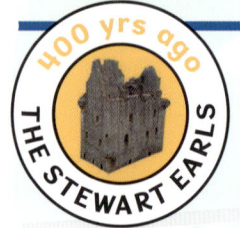
400 yrs ago — THE STEWART EARLS

David's P4 class at Scalloway School (2018/19) helped him research the Stewart Earls.

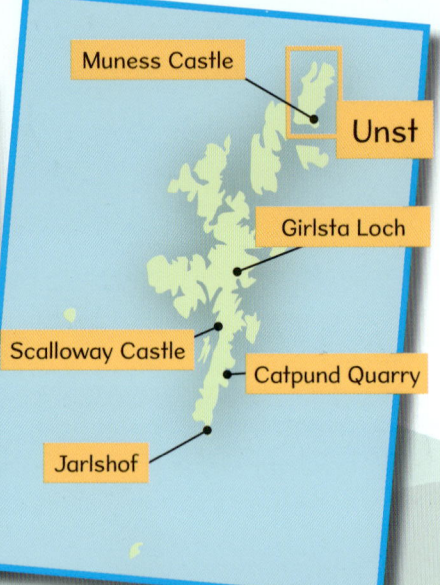
Muness Castle — Unst
Girlsta Loch
Scalloway Castle
Catpund Quarry
Jarlshof

In 1564 **Mary Queen of Scots** gave her half brother, Robert Stewart, royal estates on Orkney and Shetland. Robert died in 1593 and his son Patrick became the second Earl of Orkney and Lord of Shetland. In 1599 he began to build the Scalloway Castle. It is said that Earl Patrick was a cruel man as he taxed every parish in Shetland and forced them to send men to build the castle. To make the mortar, which holds the stones together, it is rumoured that Earl Patrick used thousands of birds eggs mixed with human hair. None of the men who built the castle were paid! He was arrested in 1609 and executed with his son in Edinburgh in 1615.

**Scalloway Castle** is an interesting place to visit with lots of rooms to explore. On the ground floor there is a kitchen where you can still see the well used for getting water. On the first floor there is a large hall and it is fun to imagine what it would have been like with people feasting and dancing.

The only other castle in Shetland is **Muness Castle** in Unst. It is the most northerly castle in the Britain. It was built for in 1598 for Laurence Bruce who was a half brother to Earl Robert Stewart.

**Tick if you made it!**

- Catpund Quarry ○
- Jarlshof ○
- Viking Unst ○
- Girlsta Loch ○
- Scalloway Castle ○
- Muness Castle ○

# Houses & Homes

Tove Matthew and her family helped research houses and homes.

The Croft House Museum at **Dunrossness** is a great place to see what a traditional Shetland house looked like. It was built around 1850 with materials that were found locally. The "ben end" is the single bedroom where the whole family slept!

Thatching the roof of East House on Burra Isle

Old agricultural tools

Spinning by the fireside around 1905-1910

### DID YOU KNOW?

Today we hope for good sailing weather as most of the food we buy in the shops arrives in Shetland by boat. At one time families grew their own food and hoped for good weather so the harvest was plentiful.

"I am going to put a pot in my new bedroom with soil in it. I am going to plant something and watch it grow." Tove.

Tove's family are building a lovely new house at Sellivoe. The materials used to build the house arrive on a lorry and they mostly come from outwith Shetland.

Tove shows us the pipes that will be used in the heating system for her house.

A Shetland house 250 years ago was very different to the houses we have today. People made their own homes, the walls were made of stone and the roofs were made of straw or turf. All the materials used to build houses were found locally. People treasured driftwood found on beaches as well as wood from shipwrecks because there were not many trees in Shetland to provide timber.

Houses were very small and usually split into two rooms. The "ben end" was the bedroom where the whole family slept; often grandparents too! The "butt end" was the kitchen and living area. A peat fire provided heat for the house as well as for cooking meals.

People and animals lived together and each house had land for keeping animals and growing crops. Families had to grow their own food and bake their own bread because there were no supermarkets. The main crops were barley and oats and from 1730 people in Shetland grew potatoes. During the summertime the men were fishing and the women and children kept the crofts running by looking after the animals and crops as well as gathering peats for the fire and knitting.

From the 1600s wealthy men called "lairds" began buying land in Shetland. Many lairds were very cruel and charged the people who lived on their land (tenants) a lot of money (rent). Lairds began to force their tenants to fish for them and if they refused they sometimes threatened to take their home away from them.

In 1886 The Crofters' Holdings Act was passed in Scotland which meant that crofters and their families could not be evicted from their homes by the greedy lairds.

Today our houses are very different! We have a bigger variety of house styles and most of the materials we use to build our homes comes from outwith Shetland.

Most houses nowadays have more than one bedroom and many children now share a bedroom with their brothers and sisters, or have a bedroom all to themselves.

Our houses now have electricity, which gives us heat and light as well as the ability to power devices such as washing machines and televisions. Nowadays we have running water and inside toilets; we can enjoy having warm showers and baths.

Most families do not have animals unless they are pets. We now get most of our food from shops so we no longer need to keep a cow for milk or grow crops for cereal or bread.

# Crofts Today

**Burland Croft Trail:** Telephone 01595 880430
**The Outpost:** www.facebook.com/TheOutpostShetland/
**Garths Croft:** Instagram @garthscroftbressay

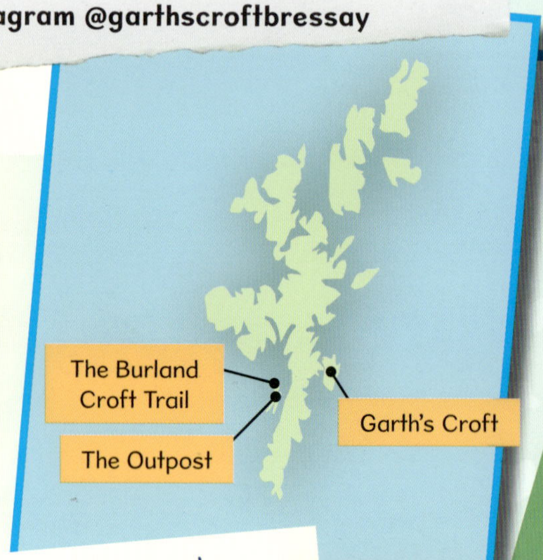

### THE OUTPOST

### BURLAND CROFT TRAIL

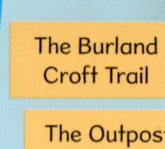

Mary and Tommy Isbister have looked after Burland Croft since 1979. Over the years they have welcomed many groups and families who come to see their friendly animals. If you visit the Burland Croft Trail you will see sheep, Shetland ponies, cows, pigs, hens, ducks and maybe even a turkey! The croft is open for visitors daily from mid May-September. Large groups need to contact Mary to arrange a suitable time for their visit. A small amount is charged for group bookings.

Read all about Bobby's adventure at the Burland Croft Trail in Valerie Watt's book

### GARTHS CROFT

On the island of Bressay you will find Garths Croft which is a traditional smallholding run by Chris Dyer. The croft has lots of interesting breeds of animals such as Iron Age pigs! Chris also grows fruit and vegetables. You can contact Garths Croft to arrange a guided tour.

Dave Cox is from Australia and has set up an Outpost on East Burra. His croft has unusual creatures for Shetland such as emus and wallabies. Children can visit anytime to feed the animals with the food provided and there is a donations box to help with the upkeep of the croft.

## Tick if you made it!

- Burland Croft Trail ○
- The Outpost ○
- Garths Croft ○

# The Shetland Bus

Joahnny Bruce helped to research the Shetland Bus.

You can learn a lot about the Shetland Bus at the Scalloway Museum. Joahnny visited the museum and learned that the Shetland Bus was actually a lot of fishing boats that went between Shetland and Norway during the Second World War. Between 1939 and 1945 Britain and its allies were at war with Germany. The Shetland Bus began because Germany had invaded and occupied Norway and the people of Shetland wanted to help the Norwegians. The fishing boats smuggled many items such as radios and ammunition across the North Sea to help the Norwegians. The boats also took Norwegian refugees to safety in Shetland.

The conditions for the men who operated the Shetland Bus were very dangerous. The weather was often stormy and the boats regularly travelled in fierce winds and huge waves. To avoid being seen by the Germans the boats also had to travel in darkness. Some of the boats were sunk or captured by the Germans. After many men lost their lives in the Shetland Bus they used sub chasers instead of fishing boats. Sub Chasers were small, fast naval vessels from the USA.

In Scalloway there is a memorial to the Shetland Bus. It is made from stones gathered from Shetland and Norway. The Norwegian stones come from the home area of each of the 44 men who lost their lives. The stones from Shetland come from places in Shetland that were involved in the Shetland Bus including Scalloway, Kergord and Lunna. The stones symbolise the enduring friendship between Shetland and Norway.

### Tick if you made it!

- The Shetland Bus Memorial, Scalloway ○
- Scalloway Museum ○
- Lunna ○

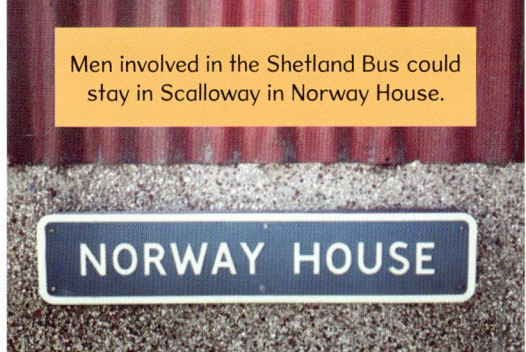

Men involved in the Shetland Bus could stay in Scalloway in Norway House.

Joahnny and a group of children from Scalloway school laid a wreath at the Shetland Bus memorial on the 17th May, 2019, to mark Norwegian Independence Day.

Joahnny visited the Scalloway Museum and saw a model of a sub chaser called KVM *Vigra* which was used in the Shetland Bus operations.

# St Ninian's Treasure

*Prasheeta Saravanan helped to research the St Ninians treasure.*

In 1958 a Lerwick schoolboy called Douglas Coutts first discovered a hoard of silver items at the chapel on St Ninian's Isle. Most of the pieces are thought to be Pictish and could be up to 1200 years old. The collection has become known as the St Ninian's Isle treasure.

The treasure is made up of 28 pieces of silverware. It was found in a wooden box under a slab which was marked with a cross. Among the treasure were 12 brooches carved with Celtic patterns. It is thought that the treasure was hidden in the church to keep it safe from Viking raiders. The treasure is now held at the National Museum of Scotland in Edinburgh. You can see a replica in Lerwick at the Shetland Museum and Archives.

### Tick if you made it!

- St Ninian's Chapel ⭘
- Replica treasure in Shetland Museum ⭘
- Real treasure in Museum of Scotland ⭘

This is the chapel site on St Ninian's Isle where the treasure was discovered in 1958.

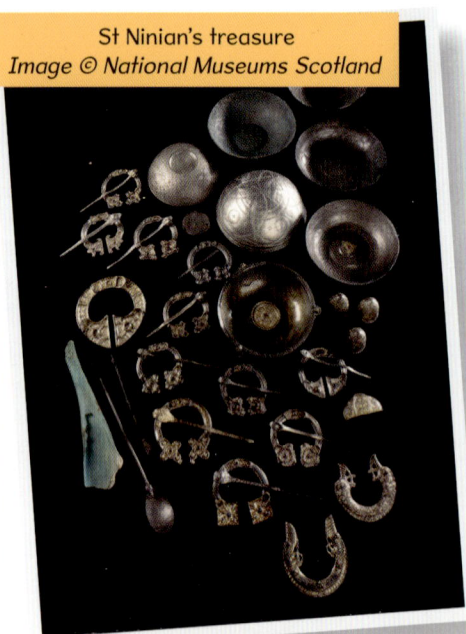

St Ninian's treasure
*Image © National Museums Scotland*

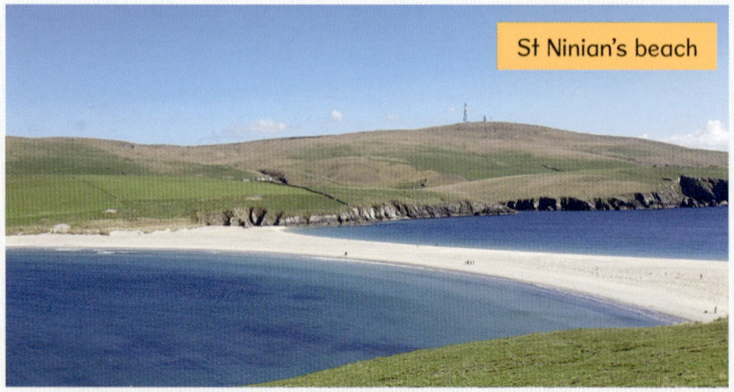

St Ninian's beach

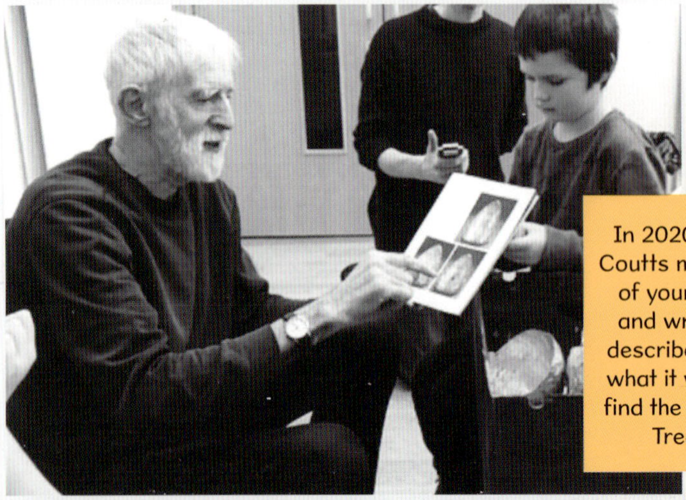

In 2020 Douglas Coutts met a group of young artists and writers and described to them what it was like to find the St Ninian's Treasure!

## THE MYSTERY OF THE PORPOISE BONE

The St Ninian's treasure was found in a wooden box made of larch which did not grow in Shetland at the time the treasure was hidden. Inside the box there were 28 silver items and a bone from a porpoise's jaw. Can you write a story or draw a picture of where the treasure came from and solve the mystery of why there was a porpoise bone in a box made of larch?

# Past & Present

## TOYS

For thousands of years children made their own toys with natural materials and everyday items which were found on or around the croft. Sticks, stones, kale stalks and bones were some of the things that were made into playthings. David made a windy craa, which was a toy that children in Shetland used to make before factory produced toys. It is made by sticking feathers into a tattie (potato). You can either throw the windy craa in the air and watch it spin, or you can pack it tightly with feathers and see it roll along the ground like a feathery ball.

Nowadays toys are made from lots of different materials. Many toys are made of plastic and are mass produced in factories. Recently people have realised that plastic is not good for the environment and there are many people beginning to use natural materials again to make toys.

## PARKING PLACES

At one time there were no roads in Shetland and the main way people travelled was by boat. Families who owned boats used "noosts" to park their boat when they were not using them. The photograph shows a boat noost in Fair Isle.

Today most people travel around Shetland by car and we put our vehicles in car parks when we are not using them.

## BUTTER

At one time people made butter by hand which took a long time. It was valuable and people traded with it. To preserve the butter people buried it in peat as it acted like a natural fridge. The photograph shows a huge lump of butter that was found in a peat hill in Yell. It is thought to have been in the peat bog since medieval times.

Today butter is made by machines in a dairy. Shetland has a dairy in Lerwick which uses milk from local cows to make its produce. The butter is put in packaging and sold in local shops. When we take butter home we put it in the fridge to keep it cool.

## CAMERAS

David is standing next to an old plate camera in the Scalloway Museum. It was invented and made in the late 1900s – over 100 years ago. It is a studio camera which means that people went to have their photographs taken at the photographer's studio and he or she would develop the images over several days with special chemicals.

Today most people carry cameras in their pockets as they are built into their mobile phones. You can edit your own photos with filter apps and send or print images instantly over the internet.

## BABY'S MILK BOTTLES

The Scalloway Museum has a baby's bottle made of glass. It was invented in the late 1800s and called a "banana bottle" because of its shape. The bottle was thought to have been a hygienic invention because it was made of glass and easy to clean.

Today most bottles are made of plastic and are often cleaned using a steriliser.

## SHOES

During the 1800s people in Shetland wore shoes that were made by hand called rivlins. The shoes were made from seal skin or cowhide which meant they were waterproof and light to wear.

Today there are so many different types of footwear. Marnie Jamieson has sparkly shoes for special occasions, trainers for sports, wellies for splashing in puddles, sandals for the summer and smucks for home.

# Curious Characters

**Illustrations by Bryan Mouat**

### Barbara Pitcairn

### Hazel Tindall

### Betty Mouat

### Barbara Pitcairn

In the 1700s Barbara Pitcairn was the companion of Elizabeth Gifford of Busta. Mrs Gifford had 14 children and the oldest was John, who would inherit the Busta estate. In 1748 John and three of his brothers mysteriously drowned. Barbara Pitcairn claimed that she and John had been secretly married and that she was expecting their baby. Elizabeth Gifford was furious and after the baby was born she sent Barbara away to Lerwick.

Lady Busta raised the little boy herself and Barbara died when she was only 35. It is said that the ghost of Barbara Pitcairn still wanders the corridors of Busta House.

### Hazel Tindall

Hazel Tindall learned to knit when she was about four years old and she could knit before she could read. Hazel is one of the fastest knitters in the world.

In 2004 she went to London and won £1000 and a rose bowl in a competition against three other people to become the "world's fastest knitter". In 2008 Hazel successfully defended this title in Minneapolis where she competed against four others, including the Guinness Record holder.

### Betty Mouat

In 1886 Betty Mouat was travelling on a boat from Grutness (Sumburgh) to Lerwick. She was planning to sell her knitting and visit the doctor but the weather quickly turned bad and the boat never made it to Lerwick.

The skipper of the boat was lost at sea and the other two crew members made it back to shore in a small rowing boat, leaving poor Betty alone drifting in darkness. Nine days later the boat with Betty drifted onto a beach in Norway. Betty had survived by clinging to a rope and living off the little amount of biscuits and milk that were on board. She was taken home to Shetland via Edinburgh and became a bit of a celebrity. Queen Victoria thought that she had been so brave and sent her a letter with £20!

### Johnnie Notions

### Johnny Notions

John Williamson was born in Eshaness in about 1740. He was a genius as he invented a vaccine to stop people getting a horrid disease called smallpox. He took pus from smallpox spots and then dried it in peat smoke. He then wrapped it up and put it underground for 7-8 years! After this time Johnnie would dig up the pus and using a special instrument that he invented he would put it under the skin of his patients. From 1769 no one he treated died of smallpox. He became known as Johnnie Notions.

### Jim o' Berry

### Jim o' Berry

James Smith (Jim O' Berry) was an incredible inventor. He looked after animals at his farm in Scalloway and in his spare time he designed and made marvellous machines. Jim even made an aeroplane in his shed. He used interesting materials to make his plane including wood from bunk beds, a car engine and parts from a motorbike!

### The Gunnister Man

### The Gunnister Man

In 1951 two men were cutting peat at Gunnister when they discovered the body of a man who has become known as the Gunnister Man. He was buried with lots of things such as a knitted purse with three coins inside, woollen clothes, two caps, gloves, a wooden stick and tub, a spoon made from horn and a quill. All the things that were buried with him were so well preserved because they had been in peat. It is thought that he lived around 1700 which means his body had been in the peat for over 300 years. You can learn lots about the Gunnister man at the Tangwick Haa Museum.

### Mary – The Eagle Bairn

### Mary – The Eagle Bairn

Folklore tells us that in the 1700s a couple were working outside on their croft in Unst. While they worked, their baby Mary, was wrapped in a shawl and lying in the field beside her parents. It is said that an eagle swooped down and carried Mary over the sea to the island of Fetlar! A local boy (12 years old) was winched down a cliff to look for baby Mary. He found her alive and well in a nest with two eagles. It is said that years later the same boy married Mary and today some people claim to be descendants of the Eagle Bairn!

# School 1+1=

Mrs Mikolajczak and her class at Hamnavoe school helped us compare a modern day classroom with a classroom 100 years ago!

A class at Hamnavoe School taken around 1912.

A classroom at Hamnavoe School taken on 1st November, 2019.

This photograph was taken just over 100 years ago and shows children looking very serious and some of them even have bare feet. Many of the children may have never seen a camera before and they would have been wondering what getting a photograph was going to be like. Many families could not afford to buy their children shoes and they had to come to school with bare feet. If you look at all the desks you will see that they are bolted to the floor so they could not be moved. The windows were deliberately set high so that the children could not see out of them and be distracted from their lessons. Many subjects were taught using a method called "rote learning" where children memorised facts by repeating them over and over again.

This photograph shows a very different classroom where the teacher is delivering a lesson using modern methods. Mrs Mikolajczak (teacher) can move the desks into different groups depending on what she is teaching, she sometimes kneels on the floor to join in the tasks. It was interesting to see that instead of a blackboard there was a whiteboard and children used paper and ipads for taking notes and learning. The classroom has big windows that the children can see out of. There is also a door which opens out to a garden which is often used as an extension of the classroom.

**DID YOU KNOW?** Slates were used in the classroom until they were replaced by paper in the 1930s

### There are now 29 schools in Shetland

- 22 primary schools
- 5 junior high schools
- 2 high schools
(1 with primary department)

### School with the most pupils

The Anderson High School in Lerwick with 915 pupils.

### School with the least pupils

Fetlar Primary School with 1 pupil.

At one time children did not have to go to school and often parents preferred children to stay at home to help with all the jobs that needed doing on the croft. The Education Act of 1872 meant all children had to go to school but many families could not afford the fees. In 1889 education became free but as there were no proper roads many children still could not go to school. Nowadays it is much easier for children to get to school as we have better roads and transport.

"I am the only child at Fetlar Primary School. It can be hard sometimes without a friend to play and work with. On a Thursday I go to Unst school and I have to go on a ferry. Fetlar school is small but Unst school is big and has lots of children. I have some nice friends that I can play and have fun with when I go. I love living on Fetlar, it is a magical place and you can have lots of adventures on the different beaches. I would like more children to live on Fetlar." Darcy Cook, age 8

## HOME EDUCATION

"There are some children who are home educated in Shetland. We like to meet up and do fun things together. We like home education because we get to learn in ways that suit us best and learn about all the things we are really interested in !" Ali Laver.

# Fishing & the Sea

Sumburgh Head Lighthouse, Visitor Centre and Nature Reserve.
www.sumburghhead.com
The Swan: www.swantrust.com/ 01595 695193

A sixareen

Serene – Pelagic trawler

Craig, Kayla Marie and their teddy at the mussel lines

Sumburgh Lighthouse

Happyhansel school learning the ropes on the Swan

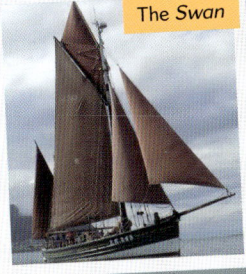
The Swan

Aaff to catch mackerel in Geordie's boat

Hansi on grandad's boat

Oscar Charlie and the Lifeboat

**DID YOU KNOW?** The fish markets in Lerwick and Scalloway land more whitefish than all of the fishing ports in England, Wales and Northern Ireland combined!

Shetland is surrounded by the sea, the west coast of Shetland looks towards the Atlantic Ocean and the east coast faces the North Sea. It is an amazing fact that Shetland's fishing and aquaculture industries make up 50% of the local economy!

People have come from all over the world to be part of Shetland's fishing industry. From around 1450 German traders came to Shetland in the summer – they set up trading böds and sold goods in exchange for fish.

About 400 years ago Dutch fishermen began to come to Shetland to fish for herring. Before the Dutch came there were no houses in Lerwick and Scalloway was the capital of Shetland. Lerwick grew due to all the trade the herring industry brought. At times there were so many herring boats in Lerwick harbour that it is said you could walk over them and almost get to Bressay!

In 1900 the Swan was built and it was the largest sail herring drifter built in Shetland. The Swan has been restored and is used for sailing training and sea adventures with groups such as youth clubs and schools.

The methods of fishing have changed over the centuries. In the 1700s Shetlanders developed the "sixareen" boat (meaning six oared). It was a wooden boat with one square sail. A crew of six men would row about 40 miles to the "haaf" (old Norse word meaning "deep sea"). The crew would set long fishing lines with hundreds of baited hooks and wait overnight for a catch. The haaf fishing was hard and dangerous work. In 1881 58 men were at the haaf lost their lives in a storm. It became known as the "Gloup disaster" as many of the men who died came from Gloup in Yell. A similar fishing disaster hit Delting in 1900 and is known as the "Delting disaster".

The boats and methods used to catch fish today are very different. Shetland now has nine pelagic trawlers which are huge fishing boats, these super trawlers fish the pelagic waters (open sea) for oily fish such as herring and mackerel. One pelagic trawler can catch the same amount of fish as 100 old herring drifters. Nowadays we also have salmon and mussel farms which you can see in sheltered areas around the coast of Shetland.

Keeping fishermen safe is important and in 1821 the first lighthouse was built at Sumburgh. At one time lighthouse keepers lived at the lighthouses as when there was a storm the light had to be lit by hand. Today the lighthouses are all automated which means no one needs to stay in them. Sumburgh lighthouse now has a visitor's centre where you can learn all about its fascinating history and press the foghorn button! The coastguard is on call all the time and sometimes you can see their helicopter called "Oscar Charlie" practicing winching people off boats. Shetland has two lifeboat stations, one in Lerwick and the other in Aith, they protect the waters on the east and west coast of Shetland.

Ability Shetland have a boat called the Wootton Lass based at Lerwick Marina that is able to accommodate wheelchairs and those with mobility issues. They also have a hoist at the marina for wheelchair users. Short sightseeing or fishing trips around the harbour are available for families free of charge and the boat is available all year round subject to weather.

For more information contact Ability Shetland on **07895 406005**, or to find out more about Ability Shetland and what else they do you can visit their website **www.abilityshetland.com** or find them on Facebook.

# Transport

Drawings and quotes by Arulaa, Kashi & Bodhi Mundair

"Shetland has many different forms of transport. We have big and small ferries, planes, trucks, buses, cars, bikes and ponies... but we don't have trains!"

Shetland is made up of about 300 islands and until roads were built in the 1800s the main way of travelling was by boat. Many people owned small boats for fishing and for travelling from one island to another.

From 1877 until 1975 a boat called the *Earl of Zetland* transported passengers and goods from Lerwick to the North Isles twice a week. The first *Earl of Zetland* ran for 68 years! In 1975 Shetland's inter island ferry service began and now there are 12 ferries taking passengers to and from the isles.

On land people walked or travelled on horses and ponies. The first road in Shetland was a gun track in Lerwick. It was built in 1781 and went from Fort Charlotte to the Knab. The first inland road was built in 1797 and it ran from Lerwick to Tingwall.

During 1971 the bridges to Trondra and Burra were completed and life changed a lot for the people that lived on these islands. Today most people travel around Shetland by car or bus.

The Islander aeroplane flies from Tingwall airport and takes people, mail and goods to the outer isles such as Fair Isle, Foula, Skerries and Papa Stour.

If you want to travel out of Shetland then you can sail from Lerwick on one of the Northlink ferries. It takes 14 hours for the boat to get to Aberdeen and it is fun having a cabin so you can sleep as you cross the North Sea. You can also get to mainland Scotland, Orkney or Norway by plane from Sumburgh airport.

Jeemsie, Aodee and Ryley show us the cabin where they slept during their 14 hour crossing to Aberdeen!

You can drive your car onto the ferry that goes to Aberdeen

Gutcher, Belmont, Ulsta, Hamar's Ness, Walls, Toft, Foula, Lerwick, Tingwall Airport (Inter island flights), Bressay, Grutness, Fair Isle

Loganair plane – Sumburgh Airport

"The buses are brilliant. You can get to most places by bus. The number 9 bus goes from Walls to Lerwick."

The *Earl of Zetland*

### DID YOU KNOW?
**1927** The first bus began to run in Shetland.
**1933** The first plane landed at Sumburgh airport.
**1975** The inter island ferry service began.

Whalsay ferry, *Linga*

Thea & Malin took the Islander plane to Foula

## Have you travelled by...
- Boat ○
- Foot ○
- Car ○
- Bus ○
- Bike ○
- Inter-island ferry ○
- Ferry to Aberdeen/Orkney ○
- Inter-island flight ○
- Plane to mainland ○

# Coming & Going

**Arulaa, Kashi and Bodhi Mundair have contributed to some of this page along with their mum, Raman Mundair.**

People have always come from around the world to live and work in Shetland. Around 1200 years ago Norse settlers arrived and 600 years ago German traders came bringing many new and useful goods to Shetland. Lerwick might not be here today if it was not for the arrival of Dutch fishermen and the herring industry 400 years ago. Sometimes people like Shetland so much that they decide to stay and make it their home and they become an important part of the community. Many children born in Shetland have parents who come from other countries; they are part of an exciting new generation of Shetlanders with rich cultural traditions.

People have also left Shetland to find work and settle all around the world. From 1865 an emigration phase began and 2000 Shetlanders left the islands in 20 years. Many people went from Shetland to Australia, New Zealand and Canada. At one time if you left Shetland you were very unlikely to return. It took months to sail to the other side of the world and travelling then was much more dangerous. Today many people travel to and from Shetland regularly and it is much easier to come back!

The majority of our relations live in southern India and we visit them every two years.

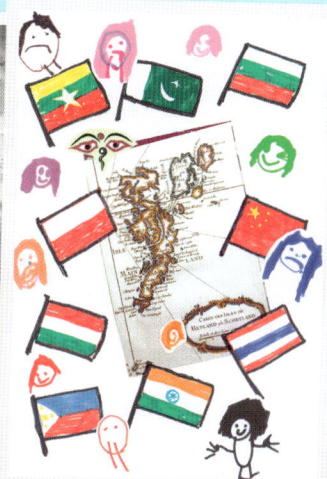

"Did you know that there was a doctor from India who lived and worked in Scalloway from 1900-1912? His name was Dr De Sylva. He married and built a house in Scalloway called Dinapore - the house is still there today. He helped many people and was responsible for the health and wellbeing of many Shetlanders. He was also a snazzy dresser!"

*Arulaa, Kashi and Bodhi Mundair.*

"My name is Sasha. I am six and I came to Shetland two years ago. My Dad is Spanish and my Mum is Russian, so it's difficult for me to learn English. I feel at home in Shetland. I love Michael's Wood – the dinosaurs are so scary - and I enjoy cycling in the park in Lerwick. I also like Up-Helly-A' and the sea. When I become a grown-up I will make a cycling tour all over Shetland as quick as I can!"

*Sasha*

"My brother Torafn and I are from Asta in the Tingwall Valley (Shetland). Now we live in Quadra Island, British Columbia, Canada. We like to go to Rebecca Spit Provincial Park, it's kind of like St Ninian's Isle but with way more trees! The beach is covered in driftwood. I miss my friends and cousins in Shetland but I really like Quadra too."

*Magnus Leask*

"My parents are from India and I was born at the Gilbert Bain Hospital in Lerwick, my brother was born in Aberdeen. The majority of our relations live in southern India and we visit them every two years. I love spending time with my grandparents, aunties, uncles and cousins. Most of them speak Tamil and I try my best to learn the basic words. At the end of each holiday I have always learned a lot more Tamil words. We never feel cold when we go to southern India.

I love living in Shetland. I like my school, friends and all the after school clubs I go to. There are no insects like mosquitoes to worry about in Shetland. Whenever I get a chance I wear my Indian clothes and people say how my Indian dresses are so colourful and full of patterns. India has a lot of colourful festivals but I do love celebrating Christmas and Up-Helly-A'."

*Prasheeta Saravanan*

23

**Shetland has its own dialect. It includes words from old Norse and Scots as well as English. Can you use any Shetland words when describing this picture?**

Gilly Bridle is an artist who lives and works in Shetland. She created this beautiful paper cut picture.

# Shetland Dialect

For more information on Shetland dialect contact Shetland ForWirds: www.shetlanddialect.org.uk

## Everyday words

Peerie – Small
Muckle – Large
Gansey – knitted jumper
Toorie – woolen cap/hat
Smucks – Slippers
Pooch – pocket
Twartree – two or three
Baa – ball
Moorit – brown
Lug – ear
Essikert – bin lorry (refuse vehicle)
Scöl – school
Da streen – last night

## About the house

Hame – home
Hoose – house
Briggistanes – footpath or flat stones laid in front of a house
Röf – roof
Lum – chimney
Böl – bed
Kist – chest
Press – cupboard
Cloot – cloth, dishcloth
Bruck – refuse, useless material
Maet – food
Gruel – porridge
Nyook – corner

## Outdoors

Girse – grass
Kokkaloorie – daisy
Banks flooer – sea pink
Banks – cliffs
Plootsh – paddle
Shoormal – shimmering light reflected on the sea
Mareel – the waters edge
Toon or rig – field
Tushkar – a spade/ tool for cutting paets
Skyumpie – large mossy bit of paet
Kishie – basket (often used for carrying paet)
Crub – small circular stone enclosure for growing cabbage
Caa – hearding or driving sheep
Yoal – small six oared boat
Blinkie – flashlight or torch

## Creatures

Shalder – Oyster catcher
Tirrick – Arctic Tern
Tammie norie – puffin
Laverick – Skylark
Skorie – seagull
Corbie – raven
Kettlins – kittens
Whalp – puppy
Yewe – ewe
Coo or Kye (plural) – cow
Grice – pig
Dratsie – otter
Neesik – porpoise
Selkie – seal
Drummic Bee – bumble bee
Scaddieman's head – sea urchin
Grottie buckie – type of cowrie shell

## The Weather and Seasons

Hairst – harvest time
Voar – spring time
Simmer dim – the twilight of a summer evening
Haily puckle – hail stone
Moorie or blind moorie – blizzard or snow storm

## Actions, feelings and emotions

Rig – to dress, get your clothes on
Bigg – to build
Dell – to delve or dig (to dell up tatties)
Blyde – glad
Filsket – high spirited, full of fun
Scunnered – fed up
Gaff – laugh
Pleepsit – always complaining
Pör aamos – frail
Tirn – angry, bad tempered
Spaegie – muscle pain and cramps caused by over exertion
Slester – to make a mess
Shew – sew
Claggy – sticky
Fant – very hungry
Sheeksfoo – mouthful
Smoorikin – kiss
Shilpet – sour
Hansel – gift

## Knitting Words

Oo – wool
Ooie – woolly
Hentilagets – tufts of wool that have come off a sheep that you find in fields or stuck to fences.
Wirset – woolen yarn
Makkin – knitting
Wires – Knitting needles
Makkin belt – knitting belt
Clew – ball of wool

**DID YOU KNOW?**

The Shetland Gruffalo was translated by Laureen Johnson and published by Itchy Coo (check out their other stories in Shetland dialect).

# Folklore

Joahnny and Raffie Bruce researched Shetland folklore and contributed the character information and magical illustrations.

Shetland is rich in folklore which are traditional stories passed down from one generation to another. In the past people often told each other folk stories as they contained shared beliefs and superstitions — they were also used to teach bairns lessons! Shetland folklore has some very interesting characters, here are a few...

After reading Da Fielnadringa Trows, Jeemsie, Aodee and Ryley went on an adventure to see if they could spot any trows!

## Trows

Trows are mystical creatures who live undergraound in "trowie knowes", they are quite peerie (small) and have pointy lugs (ears). Trows often wear gansies (knitted jumper) and walk around with bare feet. You will know when you see a trow's footprint as it will only have three toes! Trows love music so watch out for the sound of fiddles as you walk in the hills! Trows like to be cheeky and play tricks on humans. If they take you to their world for a day when you come home again you will have been away for many years as time is different in their trowie knowes.

## Njuggle

A njuggle is a horse like creature that looks a bit like a Shetland pony. It has a wheel like a tail that helps it ride very fast through the water. Njuggles are sometimes seen on land but they are never far from water. Njuggles can be mischievous and sometimes play tricks on humans.

## Selkies

A selkie is a mystical seal creature who can take off it's skin and come onto land and look like a human. There are stories of selkies marrying humans but later finding their skin and going back into the sea as their desire to be in the water was so strong, their human family were sometimes sad when they left.

## Tick if you have seen

Trow ◯    Njuggle ◯    Selkie ◯

### Look out for these two books, where you can read all about trows...

## My Shetland Folklore Story

**Design your own folklore character and write a story about its adventures. Perhaps you could include Trows, Selkies and Njuggles in your story.**

# Arts & Entertainment

What creative talent do you bring to Shetland? Do you enjoy playing an instrument, writing, drama, singing, animation, crafts, photography or something else? Shetland offers lots of opportunities for you to explore and develop your creativity. You can meet bairns who are interested in a range of art forms at the many groups that are available and there are also opportunities for individual tuition. Each year there is a drama festival run by Shetland Arts as well as a schools music festival where local groups and individuals get a chance to perform.

To find out what's on offer a good place to start is to contact **Islesburgh Community Centre** or **Shetland Arts**. Mareel is an arts centre run by Shetland Arts and it is bursting with creative opportunities. Throughout the year there are a range of workshops and short courses that offer children and opportunity to try film making, dance, writing, photography, crafts and much more. Mareel also has two cinema screens.

Bonhoga Gallery hosts the "Bairns Open" which is an annual exhibition of children's artwork and bairns are welcome to submit their masterpieces. Islesburgh Community Centre, Bonhoga Gallery and Mareel all have a cafe and they are lovely places to hang out with your friends and family. Another fun place to visit is **Aa Fired Up** which is a family friendly pottery workshop where you can decorate pottery which will be fired before you take it home to enjoy!

Shana practising piano.

Inferno Dance Group

Marni, Shana & Olivia practising for Fiddler of the Year

Creativity Club

Works of art by Shetland bairns in The Bairns Open Exhibition

Aa Fired Up

Performances by The Shetland Community School of Ballet

Islesburgh Community Centre: www.shetland.gov.uk/islesburgh / Phone 015950745100
Aa Fired Up: www.facebook.com/AaFiredUp / Phone 01595 695355
Shetland Arts: www.shetlandarts.org / Phone 01595 745500    Shetland Library: www.shetland-library.gov.uk

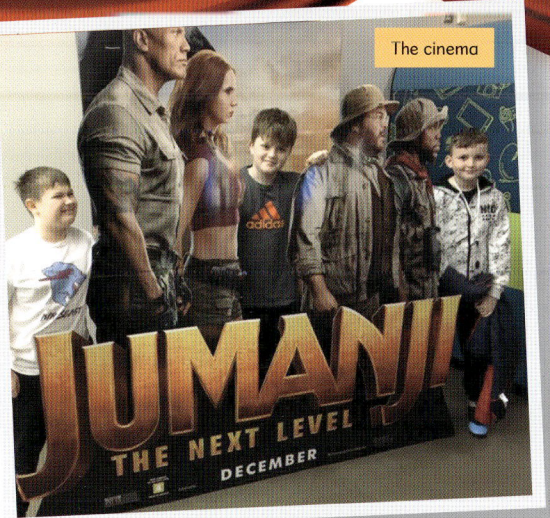
The cinema

The Shetland Library

# Be Creative!
Use this space to draw, compose a tune, write a play, design a costume, stick a photograph...

The Shetland Library is a fantastic place to visit whether you live in Shetland or are here on holiday. The library has a huge range of children's books for all ages, from baby board books right up to books for teenagers and young adults. With your library card you can take out books in foreign languages and access e-books, audio books and comics. There are loads of activities for children to take part in such as the scavenger hunts in the school holidays. You can also take on their Summer Reading Challenge and receive a medal and certificate.

The library has Bookbug sessions for 0-5 year olds. The sessions are free and open to all the family and include a mixture of songs, rhymes and stories.

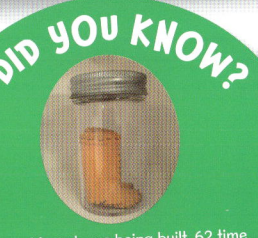
**DID YOU KNOW?** When Mareel was being built, 62 time capsules were hidden in the building. The small jars contain a hansel (gift) for the future from 62 individuals and families! Most of the capsules are buried out of sight inside the walls of the building but three can be seen in Mareel's Cafe, can you find them? What would you hide in a time capsule?

The Shetland Community Orchestra is open to musicians of all ages and abilities. It meets at the Anderson High School from 10-12 noon every Saturday during term time.

## Tick if you have tried...
- Singing ○
- Crafts ○
- Dance ○
- Writing / Reading ○
- Drama ○
- Photography / Film ○
- Playing an instrument ○
- Drawing ○
- Other creative activities ○

# Museums

www.shetlandheritageassociation.com

Oliver plays with toys from the past at the Shetland Museum and Archives.

The Tangwick Haa

The Crofthouse Museum

Whalsay Heritage Centre

The Quendale Mill

Bairns area at the Scalloway Museum

Shetland's heritage and history are brought alive in many museums and interpretive centres across the isles. The **Unst Heritage Centre** and **Boat Museum** are continually gathering artefacts and stories about life in the UKs most northerly inhabited island. You can also learn more about life in the outer isles at **The Old Haa** in Yell, the **Fetlar Interpretive Centre**, the **Whalsay Heritage Centre** as well as the the **Bressay Heritage Centre**.

At the **Tangwick Haa Museum** at Eshaness you can see a really special item – a wedding dress that is 180 years old! The dress is kept in a glass cabinet behind a curtain to protect it from light damage. The museum also tells the story of the Gunnister man.

**The Shetland Museum and Archives** in Lerwick looks after 18,000 - 20,000 historical artefacts and is a fun, interactive and child friendly place for families to visit. **The Scalloway Museum**, has an area dedicated to bringing history alive for bairns and is right next to the Scalloway Castle. **The Cabin Museum** in Vidlin has lots of information about life in Shetland and has a particular focus on Shetland's role in the two World Wars. **The Crofthouse Museum** lets you walk back in time to see what life would have been like in a crofthouse in the late 1800s. The **Quendale Water Mill** and the **Hoswick Visitors Centre** are also interesting places to visit in the South Mainland.

Most of the museums and interpretive centres are open May-September. Some of them will be open during the winter by appointment. The Shetland Museum and Archives are open all year round.

**DID YOU KNOW?**

Elin Waterhouse went to the Tangwick Haa Museum to see the wedding dress worn by Barbara Hay of Laxfirth on the 7th May, 1840. Miss Hay married Henry Cheyne of Tangwick and her dress was all hand sewn and made of pure brocaded silk.

### Tick if you made it!

- Unst Heritage Centre & Boat Museum ○○○
- Fetlar Interprative Centre ○○○
- Whalsay Heritage Centre ○○○
- Hoswick Visitors Centre ○○○
- Scalloway Museum ○○○
- The Old Haa ○○○
- The Cabin Museum ○○○
- Shetland Museum & Archives ○○○
- Bressay Heritage Centre ○○○
- Crofthouse Museum ○○○
- Quendale Water Mill ○○○
- Tangwick Haa ○○○

# Peerie Lavericks Song

Words: **Maria Barclay**   Music: **Traditional**

Louie Coyne enjoying singing 'Peerie Lavericks'

See da peerie laverick
(All children curl up in a ball)
In da lift abun
Shush, will we lissen (Shush sign)
Tae his happy tune

Up abun, whit a boney tune (Point up)

Sing peerie laverick
Sing, Sing, Sing
Sing peerie laverick
Sing, Sing, Sing
Sing peerie laverick
Sing, Sing, Sing
Sing, Sing
Sing, Sing, Sing

See da peerie drummy-bees
(All children curl up in a ball)
In da perks in June
Will we try and woken dem
We wir happy tune?

De're so still, are dey ill?

Buzz peerie drummy bees (Jump up)
Buzz, Buzz, Buzz
Buzz peerie drummy bees (Jump up)
Buzz, Buzz, Buzz
Buzz peerie drummy bees
Buzz, Buzz, Buzz
Buzz, Buzz
Buzz, Buzz, Buzz

See da peerie laverick
(All children curl up in a ball)
In da lift abun
Shush, will we lissen (Shush sign)
Tae his happy tune

Up abun, whit a boney tune (Point up)

Sing peerie laverick
Sing, Sing, Sing
Sing peerie laverick
Sing, Sing, Sing
Sing, Sing
Sing, Sing, Sing

Sing peerie laverick (Jump up)
Sing, Sing, Sing
Sing peerie laverick
Sing, Sing, Sing
Sing peerie laverick (Jump up)
Sing, Sing, Sing
Sing, Sing
Sing, Sing, Sing

'Laverick' is the Shetland name for a 'Skylark'

**Draw your own peerie laverick in the space below:**

### Glossary – "What da Wirds Mean"

- abun – above
- boney – bonnie
- drummy-bees – bumble bees
- lift abun – sky above
- peerie laverick – small skylark
- perks – parks/fields
- woken – waken

# Festivals, Shows & Celebrations

Up-Helly-A' evening torchlit procession

Up-Helly-A' day procession

> "I was in the Jarl Squad in 2016. I was six. My favourite memories are paining the galley, practicing the songs and marching, singing in the Toll Clock shopping centre, sitting in the Town Hall, being appreciated, sitting in the galley and watching the galley burn."
> *Adam Leslie (age 10)*

**DID YOU KNOW?**

Lesley Simpson became the first female Jarl on the 13th March, 2015, at the South Mainland Up-Helly-A'. She chose to be "Aud the Deep Minded" from the Norse sagas.

People in Shetland know how to have a good party with music and dancing. Each spring musicians come from all around the world to take part in the annual Shetland Folk Festival. During this weekend there are fun musical workshops for children as well as the annual "Peerie Spang".

Shetland has a fantastic fire festival called Up-Helly-A' which takes place each year on the last Tuesday of January. The evening procession is a sight to be seen, squads of guizers wear fancy dress costumes and carry flaming torches in a set route around the streets of Lerwick. The first Up-Helly-A' torch lit procession took place in 1881 and it had 60 torches.

In recent years the average number of guizers taking part in the procession is 980! The chief guizer and leader of the procession is called the Guizer Jarl and his squad dress as Vikings to celebrate Shetland's Norse heritage. Two of the big secrets of the festival are what costumes the jarl squad will wear and what the name and design of the galley ship will be.

At the end of the evening procession the guizers throw their flaming torches into the galley and the boat is burnt. Various communities in Shetland have smaller fire festivals based on Up-Helly-A' which take place from January until the end of March.

During the summer months some communities in Shetland host agricultural shows where there is so much to see and do. It is interesting to see all the animals and farm equipment such as tractors and machinery. You can enter competitions in all sorts of categories such as baking and crafts. The best bit is all the yummy food as well as the fun rides.

Each year Lerwick has a colourful and family friendly mid summer carnival where people and decorated floats parade through the streets of Lerwick.

Each area of Shetland has different ways of celebrating events such as weddings and New Year. An old wedding custom in Shetland is for a fiddler to lead the bride, groom and wedding party in a procession to the church. At New Year some people go "guizing" and wear masks when they visit their friend's houses. The guizers try to be be the "first foot" (first visitor of the year) at each house they visit and their friends have to guess who they are!

A wedding procession in Yell

The "Peerie Spang" at the Folk Festival

Country Show

# Knitting

People from all over the world buy Shetland wool and knitwear. About 400 years ago many Dutch fishermen came to Shetland each summer and Shetlanders' would sell and trade their knitwear with them. Being able to make and sell knitted items was an important part of many families income and girls would learn to knit when they were young. In the 1950s the home knitting machine was introduced and you could make items faster than knitting by hand.

Shetland has its very own breed of sheep and at the Sandness Mill they use the wool from Shetland sheep to make beautiful colours of wool, which is then made into jumpers with Shetland patterns and designs.

Each autumn Shetland hosts "Wool Week" where people come from all around the world to celebrate and learn more about Shetland knitwear.

### Knitting words

- Oo – wool
- Ooie – woolly
- Wirset – woollen yarn
- Makkin – knitting
- Wires – knitting needles
- Makkin belt – knitting belt
- Clew – ball of wool
- Hentilagets – tufts of wool that have come off a sheep that you find in fields or stuck to fences.

## The Journey of wool – from sheep to yarn

1. 2. 3. 4. 5. 6.

- Sheep are sheared with electric or traditional hand clippers and the very dirty parts are removed, folded, rolled and packed into "oo bags."
- When all the sheep on the croft or farm are sheared their fleeces are taken to a wool broker or spinning mill.
- The fleeces are then graded for their quality and go through a series of 11 processes including washing, carding and spinning.
- They are then wound into balls of yarn ready for knitting.
- Shetland yarn is known particularly for its softness and warmth and is sold widely across the world.

## Shetland Peerie Makkers

The Shetland Peerie Makkers project is helping primary school aged bairns learn the special techniques and knowledge of Shetland hand knitting. The children learn to knit in small supported groups in their own community following the Shetland tradition of sharing skills across generations in a supportive environment. The groups meet each week, at lunchtime or after school and begin by learning how to knit basic stitches before moving on to design their own colourful creations. The young knitters use Fair Isle or Shetland lace patterns for inspiration.

### Quotes from some peerie makers:

*"They started me on fingerless gloves. I'm making a headband which has a different design on each side so when you flip it over its different."*

*"We get to speak with all our friends and we get to just enjoy doing makkin. You can mak tons of things and you'll never get bored with it."*

*"Right now we start off with something easy and then we can create our own patterns and things we want to do. You can let your mind go free and just choose what you want to create."*

*"When I show my family they are like, 'You really made that? It's cool!'."*

*"You've made it yourself and you can be proud of it. But if you go and buy something you're not like proud. But if you like finish knitting a jumper it makes you feel proud."*

Triple Tone Circular Scarf by Terri Malcolmson

**Shetland Peerie Makkers:** www.shetlandpeeriemakkers.com or www.facebook.com/shetlandpeeriemakkers/

This photograph shows two Shetland ladies knitting while they are carrying heavy kishies (baskets) of paet.

### DID YOU KNOW?

There is a style of knitting that comes from one of Shetland's islands called Fair Isle. No one knows what inspired the Fair Isle patterns or when they began but they have become famous all around the world. One of the rules of a Fair Isle pattern is that you can use no more than two colours in each row!

This Burra bear created by Wendy Inkster is made from ten different pieces of Fair Isle! Can you spot the different patterns?

## Design your own Fair Isle pattern...

# Scones & Bannocks

Hani shows us how to make scrumptious scones and Eva shares Shetland's version, yummy bannocks!

## Hani's scone recipe

### Ingredients:
450g (1lb) self-raising flour
50g (1¾ oz) caster sugar
100g (3½ oz) softened butter, cut into pieces
2 free range eggs
A little milk
2 level teaspoons of baking powder

Oven: preheat to 220°c/200°c (fan) or Gas mark 7

### Method
1. Put the flour, baking powder and sugar into a bowl.
2. Add the butter to the bowl and rub it in with your fingertips till the mixture looks like breadcrumbs.
3. Crack the eggs into a measuring jug and add enough milk to make the liquid 300ml/10 fl oz.
4. Stir the egg and milk into the bowl with the flour mixture (you might not need it all) and mix until you get a soft, sticky dough.
5. Put the dough onto a floured work surface and roll out the dough so it is 2cm thick.
6. Cut out as many scones as possible with a scone cutter or a cup.
7. Brush the top of the scones with any left over milk/egg mixture.
8. Put the scones on lightly greased baking trays and then bake them in the oven for 12-15 minutes or until the scones are risen and are a pale, golden colour.
9. Put the scones onto a wire rack to cool.

*You can eat the scones plain or fill them with jam and cream!*

## Eva shares Rosabell Halcrow's bannock recipe

### Ingredients:
8oz self-raising flour
1 teaspoon salt
200ml or 7fl. oz milk
1 teaspoon vinegar

### Method
1. Sift flour and salt.
2. Add the vinegar and milk, mix to a soft dough.
3. Roll out into two batches to make 8 bannocks.
4. Cook on top of cooker on a cooling tray or similar, elecrtic hob number 4 or electric frying pan.
5. Wrap bannocks in dish towel to keep them soft.

# Cari's Paet Story

In Shetland the winters can be cold and windy and there is nothing better to keep cosy than a good peat fire. Cari Sutherland tells us about the process of getting peat (or paet in Shetland dialect) from the hill to the fire at home.

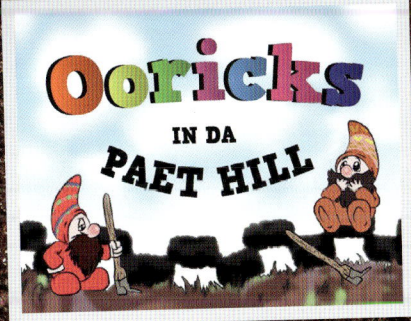

## Ooricks IN DA PAET HILL

Ann Marie Anderson has written a story about Da Oorricks adventure in da paet hill. The book is illustrated by Jenny Duncan.

Casting paets is a tradition in our family and every year I go to the paet hill and work on my own paet bank.

**1** First I flay da moor (take the top layer of heather and roots off) using a ripper and shovel, then I put da faels (fells) doon so the paets are ready to cast.

**2** I begin casting and use a tushkar to cut my paets.

**3** I then place my casted paets in a dik (dyke) so the sun can dry them and they get a good skin on them.

**Tushkar** — A spade with a feathered blade, used for cutting paets.

**4** I clear the gref (bottom of the bank) of clods (peerie paets).

**5** I ken it is time to raise da paets when they have a good skin on them. I turn da paets around so any wet eens get dried.

**6** Once they are dry it is time for baggin da paets so we can take them home. We load them in da trailer and take them home where we store them in the shed ready for the fire.

**7** A paet fire.

## DID YOU KNOW?

Many interesting items have been found in Shetland's paet hills as paet acts like a preservative. Here are a few...

**1200 years old** – fragments of a Viking glove were found in Foula.

**500 years old** – a precious stash of butter was found in the ground in Yell. Butter was a precious commodity and it is thought it was buried to keep it cool and safe.

**300 years old** – it was Cari's great grand uncle, James Johnson, who discovered the Gunnister man (see Curious Characters page) while he was digging for paets in 1951.

# Fun Places Outside

The Smuggler's Cave

The Steens of Stofast

The Burn of Lunklet

There are so many fun places to go outside and this book gives suggestions in other sections such as in Beaches and Woodlands.

## Useful websites:
www.shetland.org/things/outdoor
www.shetland.org/things/outdoor/walking/steens-of-stofast-circular
www.shetland.org/60n/blogs/posts/spelunking-in-burra

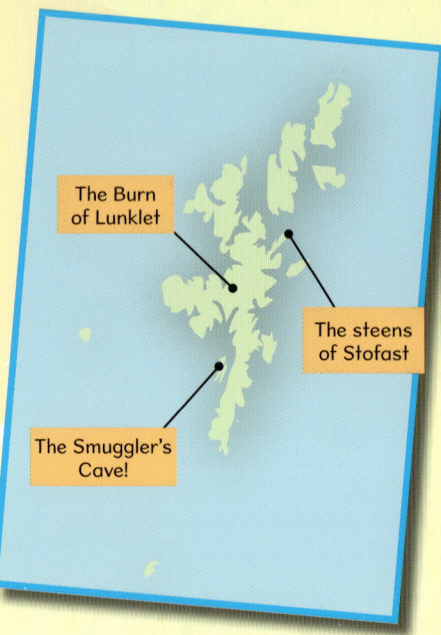

Ability Shetland have four all terrain wheelchairs, two attendant wheelchairs where the person in the chair is pushed by someone else and two self propelled chairs.

These chairs support people with physical disabilities and mobility issues to access the more difficult terrain of the isles such as beaches and coastal walks and are available to visitors free of charge.

If you would like more information about the wheelchairs contact Ability Shetland: **www.abilityshetland.com** or **phone 07895 406005.**

The Burn of Lunklet
The steens of Stofast
The Smuggler's Cave!

### DID YOU KNOW?
**GEOCACHING**
Shetland is a great place for geocaching with lots of beautiful and unusual places to find and deposit your treasures.

Shetland has so many fun places to go outside. You are never far away from a beautiful beach, place of historic interest or natural beauty. There are lots of burns and rockpools to guddle in as well as cool creatures to spot when you are out and about. Here are three favourite places to go for an adventure:

### The Smugglers Cave
Near Hamnavoe on Burra Isle there is a fantastic cave to explore. The small cave entrance is 200 metres inland and is recognisable as there is a fixed rope ladder descending into a hole in the ground. Once in the cave the sound of the sea will guide you towards the cave mouth. It is quite a tricky place to find so if you feel like an adventure there are brilliant directions at **www.shetland.org/60n/blogs/posts/spelunking-in-burra**

### The Burn of Lunklet
The Burn of Lunklet is at East Burrafirth, there are parking places and a sign to show where the path beside the burn begins. After walking for about 10 minutes you will find a little waterfall which is a great place for picnics and guddling in the burn.

### The Steens of Stofast
The Steens of Stofast are near Lunna on the north east mainland of Shetland. The Steens are huge boulders that have been dumped by a glacier during the ice age and overlook the Loch of Stofast. It is a brilliant place to walk, climb and play hide and seek. The steens are huge and it almost feels like you are in a different world when you are beside them.

## Tick if you made it!

**The Smuggler's Cave**   **The Steens of Stofast**   **The Burn of Lunklet**
○                         ○                           ○

**Add your own 'Fun places to go outside' destinations:**

.................................... ○   .................................... ○   .................................... ○

.................................... ○   .................................... ○   .................................... ○

# Beaches

**Useful website: www.shetland.org/things/explorenature/beaches**

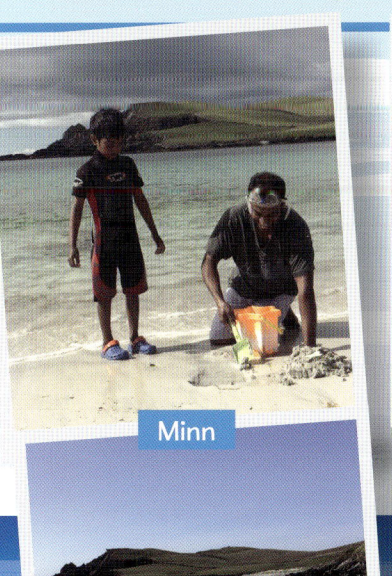

Minn

Tresta, Fetlar

St Ninians

Norwick

### DID YOU KNOW?

Alex Purbrick gathered different coloured sand from beaches all around Shetland and made a picture called a Sand Mandala. Her Mandala was for "Shundahal" which is a Shoshone word (Native American) for "peace and harmony with all creation". Can you make a picture with sand?

Breckon, West Sandwick, Skaw, Sandwick, Dale of Walls, Tresta, Sandsound, Meal, Minn, Sands of Sound, St Ninians, Reawick, Quendale, Levenwick, Spiggie, West Voe

Shetland has lots of beautiful beaches and they all have different things to offer. It is impossible to list them all but here are a few favourites:

**Skaw** — Britain's most northerly sandy beach.

**Sandwick** (Unst) and **Sands of Breckon** (Yell) — both these beautiful beaches have remains of Viking settlements.

**Reawick** — The sand is made of red granite.

**Minn** — This beach is magical, one side the beach has beautiful white sand and on the other side there is a pebbly beach, which is fantastic for skimming stones.

**St Ninian's** — The longest tombolo in Britain (500 metres) which leads to St Ninian's Isle, where Pictish treasure was found in 1958 by a Lerwick schoolboy. See page 16.

## Tick if you made it!

| | | | |
|---|---|---|---|
| Skaw, Unst ○ | Meal, Burra ○ | St Ninian's ○ | Sandwick, Unst ○ |
| Minn, Burra ○ | Quendale ○ | Breckon, Yell ○ | Reawick ○ |
| Sands of Sound ○ | West Sandwick, Yell ○ | Dale of Walls ○ | Spiggie ○ |
| Tresta, Fetlar ○ | Sandsound ○ | Levenwick ○ | West Voe ○ |

**Add your own beach destinations:**

.................................... ○  .................................... ○  .................................... ○

.................................... ○  .................................... ○  .................................... ○

# Aboot Da Banks

Elias, Zac and Phoebe Kerr went exploring aboot da banks and this is what they found...

It is good to explore the banks when it is low tide. Sometimes the rocks can be a bit slippy so take your time!

Remember to put the creatures and rocks back where you found them.

...Scaddiemans Head (Sea Urchin)

Grottie buckies are small shells that you sometimes find aboot da banks. They are said to bring good luck! Grottie buckies are also known as cowrie shells.

...Crabs

There are lots of rocky banks to explore around the coast of Shetland. Keep and eye out for...

...Limpets

...Starfish

...Sea Anemone

...Seaweed

...Hermit Crabs

# Woodlands

For more information about Shetland's woodlands contact the Shetland Amenity Trust www.shetlandamenity.org. Phone: 01595 694688

Kergord Rope Swing

Voxter

"I visited Michael's Wood for the first time in over two years thanks to the all-terrain wheelchair I borrowed from Ability Shetland. I got to access the whole place and loved seeing the dinosaurs and reading all the information boards (I love facts!). I was able to get in about the trees and play with my little sister. My dad certainly worked his muscles pushing me up the hill and I loved the excitement of going down the hill really quickly."

**Harrison Morris**

## DID YOU KNOW?

Between 2018-2019 Shetland Amenity Trust germinated over 5000 trees for planting in Shetland.

**Sullom** – a small wood that is worth a visit. It has a mud kitchen for making forest feasts.

**Voxter** – an easy wood to get to and a great place for playing hide and seek. You will always find dens made from sticks and obstacle courses made from rope.

**Michael's Wood** – at this plantation you can enjoy the dinosaur trail, swings, pirate ship, teddy bear's picnic and much more. It also has a covered picnic area which is good on rainy days.

**Kergord** – a great place for adventuring, there is a lovely stream and a rope swing. You have to walk across a small field to get to the wood which is on the side of a hill.

**Da Gairdins** – the gardens were started in 1997 and over 25,000 trees and shrubs have been planted. There is a lovely variety of woodland, flower gardens and in the summer the three large ponds are full of frogs!

Michael's Wood

Da Gairdins

### Tick if you have been...

Sullom ○   Da Gairdins ○   Michael's Wood ○   Voxter ○   Kergord ○

# Art & Craft with natural materials

All around Shetland you can find natural materials which you can use to create your very own works of art...

**DID YOU KNOW?** Hentilagets are what people in Shetland call the tufts of wool that have come off a sheep that you find in fields or stuck to fences!

### Fun with Felt

The sheep in Shetland are covered in a thick fleece to keep them warm. Sometimes bits of their fleece come off and you can find it in the fields or stuck to fences. You can use this wool in many ways in your artwork such as to make felted pictures or to decorate sculptures. You can buy coloured wool for felting from the Sandness Mill.

There are two techniques for making felted pictures, these are wet felting or needle felting. One technique uses pricking the felt with a needle and the other uses soap and water to bind the wool fibres together. You can find information on making felted pictures online or from books at the library.

### Coastal Crafts

Beaches are great places to find all sorts of treasures such as different types of shells, seaweed, stones, sea glass and feathers. You can have fun making a picture or pattern with what you find.

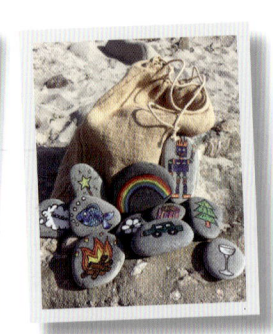

### Stone Painting

You can find stones almost anywhere. Some beaches are good for finding round, flat stones which are especially good for painting. It is good to clean the stone first and then decorate it with arcrylic paint which does not wash off.

### Woodland Creations

### Mud Pictures

Ardan and Dana went to Kergord woods and had fun using natural materials to create some woodland craft.

"We took some wool and strips of old fabric into the woods with us then we each had to find a good stick. We sat under the trees weaving memories into the stick. We looked for ferns, leaves, lichen and anything else we could find to add to our sticks. Dana made a dream stick onto which she weaved good thoughts and colourful memories."

Take some paper into the wood, soak it in a burn or any nearby water. When the paper is wet you can use your fingers or sticks, leaves and ferns to smear the mud onto the paper and see the patterns the mud makes. We found some blackberries and smeared them onto our pictures, which gave the mud a purple colour.

If you would like to learn more about playing outside with natural materials then Alex Purbrick takes small groups for outdoor rambles and art adventures. If you would like further information on workshops using natural materials contact alexpurbrick@live.com or jane_malcolm@hotmail.com

# Cool Creatures

**Roshik Saravanan helped research this page**

Shetland has so many cool creatures such as birds, fish, sea mammals and animals that live on the farms and crofts. Some creatures stay in Shetland all year round while others visit on their migratory journey. It is impossible to list all the cool creatures that live around Shetland but here are a few…

### DID YOU KNOW?
Shetland has its own subspecies of bumblebee. It is very distinctive with an orange chest and yellowish belly. Its Latin name is Bombus muscorum agricolae.

*The Hillswick Wildlife Sanctuary*
*The Sumburgh Lighthouse Visitors Centre*

## Tammie Norrie (Puffin)
Puffins are very cute and much smaller than you would imagine. They are famous for their coloured beak. You can see puffins in Shetland between April and early August and a really good place to watch them is at Sumburgh Head. Puffins breed in underground burrows and parents take turns to look after the eggs and catch fish once the chicks are hatched. It is a bit of a mystery where puffins spend the winter but it is thought they go out to sea.

## Dratsie (Otter)
Otters spend a lot of time in the water and they are good at swimming and catching fish. They have dense fur to keep them warm and webbed feet to help them swim. Otters can be quite shy and therefore can be tricky to spot, especially among the rocks and seaweed. They live in holts which are secret dens where they can safely raise their cubs.

## Shetland Pony
You can see Shetland ponies in the fields and hills all over Shetland. It is said that although Shetland ponies are small they are the strongest of all horse and pony breeds for their size. In Shetland they were used as workhorses and from the 1840s they were used in the mines of Britain to pull wagons of coal. You can have Shetland pony riding lessons and learn how to groom them and clean their hooves.

## Tirrick (Arctic tern)
When Shetlanders spot the first Arctic terns arriving they know spring has begun. You can see Arctic terns in Shetland between May and August and they are interesting to watch as they hover above the water and then suddenly dive for a fish. Arctic terns have the longest migration of all birds and fly up to 22,000 miles a year between summer in the Arctic and summer in the Antarctic. It is said that long lived tirricks "may have flown a distance equivalent to that of flying from the earth to the moon!" (Paul Harvey, *Birds of a Shetland Summer*)

## Orcas
If you are lucky you might see an orca (killer whale) swimming around Shetland. Orcas are apex predators which means that they are at the top of their food chain. One of their favourite things to eat are seals and there are plenty of those around Shetland. The grey patch behind the dorsal fin is called the "saddle" and the scars are as unique as human fingerprints. From photographs experts have matched some of the animals seen in Shetland to those recorded in Icelandic waters in winter.

## The Hillswick Wildlife Sanctuary
Sometimes seal pups and otter cubs lose their mums and need to be rescued because they can't survive on their own. That's when Hillswick Wildlife Sanctuary steps in, keeping them warm and safe and fattening them up on milk and fish until they're ready for life in the wild. It takes three months for a seal pup to be big enough to be released. Otter cubs rely on their mum until they are one year old so they stay at the sanctuary for much longer. You can see videos of what they do at the sanctuary on Facebook and their website at www.hillswickwildlifesanctuary.org. You can also visit when there are seals being looked after but always phone first on 01806 503348.

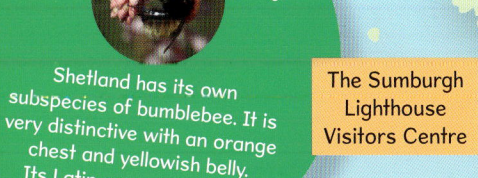

### What have you seen?
- ⭕ Tammie Norrie (Puffin)
- ⭕ Dratsie (Otter)
- ⭕ Tirrick (Arctic Tern)
- ⭕ Shetland Pony
- ⭕ Drummie Bee (Bumble Bee)
- ⭕ Orcas
- ⭕ ........................................
- ⭕ ........................................

### Places to spot cool creatures
If you look carefully you can find creatures everywhere. You can see birds and insects in your garden and during March and October Shetland often has unusual birds passing through. Can you spot any creatures out the window of your car or school bus?

If you want to learn more about creatures then the Sumburgh Lighthouse Visitors Centre has a natural history exhibition and nature activity sheets to compete. In the summer it is a great place to spot seabirds such as puffins as well as sea mammals.

Find inspiration on the RSPB website where there are activities to help wildlife, explore nature and enjoy lots of wild fun with friends and family.

The local RSPB team have been working with eight schools in Shetland to become "Nature Friendly Schools" – children design and manage their school grounds for wildlife and wild play and they are great places for a family picnic.

### Look out for
Shetland Nature Festival takes place in the summer and offers a varied programme of fun activities and workshops.

**Sumburgh Head Lighthouse, Visitor Centre and Nature Reserve:** www.sumburghhead.com
**RSPB Shetland** www.rspb.org.uk. Phone: 01950 460800
**Shetland Amenity Trust:** www.shetlandamenity.org. Phone: 01595 694688

*Shetland Nature Festival*
*rspb giving nature a home Scotland*

# Geopark

**Contact details:** Shetland Amenity Trust, Garthspool, Lerwick, Shetland ZE1 0LN
www.info@shetlandamenity.org   Phone: 01595 694688

Thea and Malin's dad, Rory Tallack, works at Shetland Amenity Trust. He is Shetland's Geopark manager. Together they tell us what it means for Shetland to be a Geopark.

## Geoparks

Our rocks and landscapes are amazing which is why the whole of Shetland is a UNESCO Global Geopark. Geoparks celebrate the fact that our nature and our culture is connected to the rocks beneath our feet. Shetland has 2700km of coastline so there are loads of places to explore Shetland's rocks – but here are a few of the best bits…

## Keen of Hamar

The Keen of Hamar in Unst looks like the surface of the moon. It hasn't changed very much since the end of the last ice age, almost 12,000 years ago. Although it looks completely bare from a distance, get down on your hands and knees and you will find loads of tiny plants growing between the stones. Some Arctic plants still grow here including Edmondston's Chickweed, which grows nowhere else in the world.

## Fossil fish

Long before there were dinosaurs on the earth there were huge mountains to the west of Shetland with rivers that flowed down into lakes. Fossils of fish that lived in these lakes can be found in several places in Shetland, but the easiest place to find them is Shingly Geo. Please don't damage or take the fossils – once they are gone, they are gone forever.

## Eshaness

The cliffs at Eshaness are very high but they were once part of a much higher volcano. Most of it has been worn away by the sea, but you can still see layer upon layer of lava flows in the cliffs which cooled down and turned into rock. Below the lighthouse the rocks are made up of boulders and smaller rock fragments that were blasted out of the volcano's crater, which was probably just offshore above the islands of Muckle Ossa and Little Ossa.

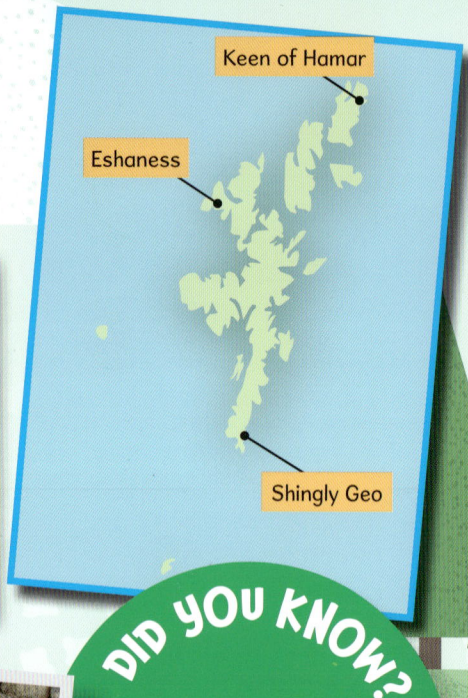

### DID YOU KNOW?

The rocks we are standing on are constantly moving, very slowly. America and Europe used to be joined together but now they are drifting away from each other at about the speed your fingernails grow!

### Tick if you've made it!

- Eshaness ⭕
- Fossil fish at Shingly Geo ⭕
- Keen of Hamar ⭕

**Add your own destinations:**

.................................................. ⭕

.................................................. ⭕

# Looking After Our Environment

**Shetland Amenity Trust:** www.shetlandamenity.org.  Phone: 01595 694688

It is good to look after our environment and we can do this by making helpful choices about the way we live and by taking part in community projects that care for our environment. For over 30 years the Shetland Amenity Trust has organised the UK's most successful litter pick up. Each year a few thousand volunteers from around Shetland take part in Da Voar Redd Up (the spring clean up) and collect rubbish from beaches, coastlines and roadsides. To find out how you, your school or community group can take part in Da Voar Redd Up you can contact the Shetland Amenity Trust.

Shetland Farm Dairies has recently introduced reusable glass bottles for its milk and hopes that this will help people reduce the amount of plastic they buy. We can be kind to the environment by buying local produce which means we reduce the "carbon footprint" of our goods.

*A community Redd Up at Woodwick beach.*

**Thank you to our 2019 Volunteers and Sponsors**

DA VOAR REDD UP 2019

- 4,500 Volunteers participated – 20% of the Shetland population
- 240 groups participated
- 1075km of land improved, an average of 2.8miles per group
- amounting to 13,500 Volunteer hours
- over 48 tonnes of rubbish collected
- worth the equivalent of £120,000 in paid work*

#DunnaChuckBruck

*based on the Scottish Living Wage

*Da Voar Redd Up 2019 Fun Facts*

*David and Roshik buying local milk in reusable glass bottles.*

## What do you do to be kind to the environment?

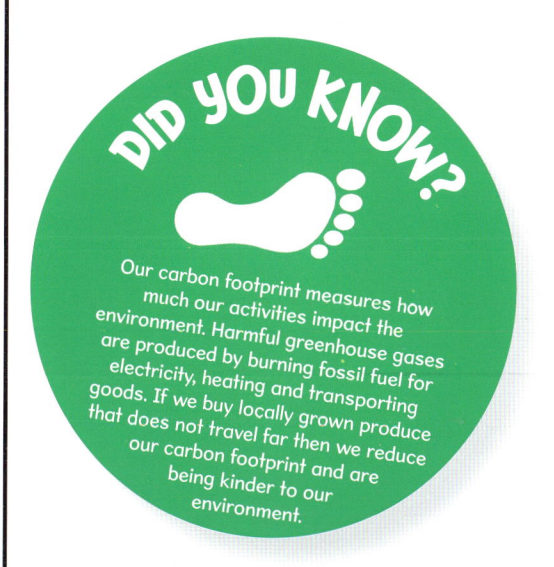

**DID YOU KNOW?**

Our carbon footprint measures how much our activities impact the environment. Harmful greenhouse gases are produced by burning fossil fuel for electricity, heating and transporting goods. If we buy locally grown produce that does not travel far then we reduce our carbon footprint and are being kinder to our environment.

43

# Parks & Gardens

**Lea Gardens:** Open daily for visitors 2-5pm (except Thursdays) from April to September. Phone: 01595 810454
**Sarah Kay's Garden:** Open daily from May to October as part of Scotland's Garden Scheme. For a guided tour of garden and art studio contact www.facebook.com/sarahkaysgarden

Shetland has over 70 fantastic playparks with a wide range of equipment such as swings, slides, zip wires, climbing frames and obstacle courses. Some of the parks also have a football pitch and a multi court. All the playparks that are on school grounds are open to the public outside of school hours.

King George V Park

Sandwick Central

Nesting Primary School

Walls

Symbister

Cunningsburgh

The Cake Cupboard, Hoswick

Hoswick play park

*Short Breaks for Children visited three playparks and this is what you found ...*

### Bigton park

The first thing that you notice when you get Bigton playpark is that it has a great view, it is also wheelchair friendly and has super high swings. The park has friendly neighbours (Shetland ponies) and is near to a shop, public toilets and St Ninians Isle beach.

### Hoswick playpark

The local community at Hoswick have created a super, unique and natural playpark, they have used a range of easily found materials and resources such as canoes, chalk boards and tyres. You can whip up some grub in the gutter kitchen and whizz down the pipe slides, the park is also near the Hoswick Visitors Centre and the Cake Cupboard.

### Nesting Primary School

You can use the Nesting School playground outside of school hours. It is famous for its outdoor learning area which includes a mud kitchen. You can follow the secret path and enjoy walking through the trees. See if you can find the Viking galley boat and have a snack at one of the picnic areas. The multi court is full of loose parts such as tyres and pipes which have been donated by local companies, there is also a smaller playpark for younger children at the front of the school.

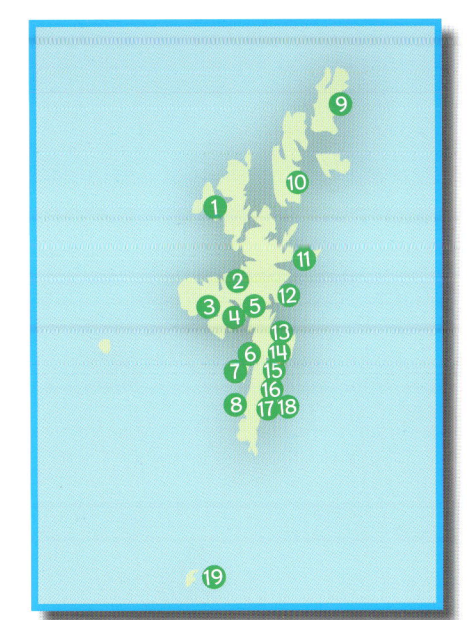

Shetland has many beautiful gardens and community spaces such as the Lerwick flower park and Mary Russland's cottage in Scalloway. The community in North Roe have made a beautiful garden which is a fun place to visit. Some private gardens are open to the public during the summer months such as Sarah Kay's Garden in Scalloway and the magical Lea Gardens on the west mainland of Shetland.

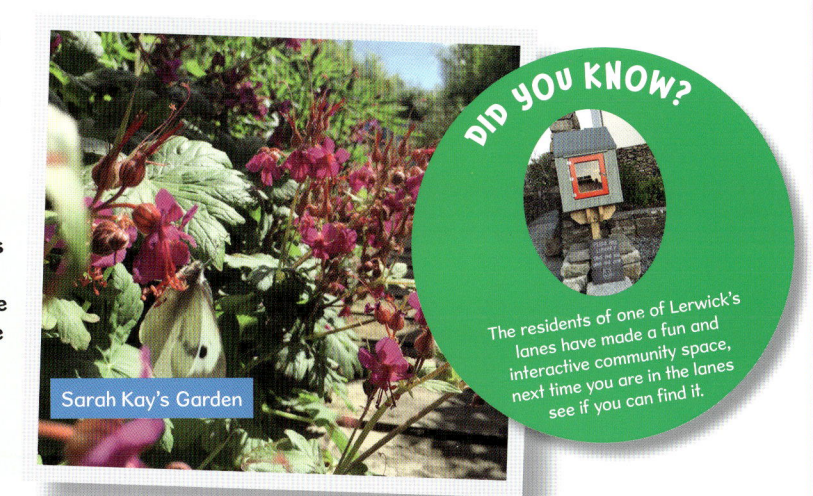

### The bairns at the North Roe school had lots of good things to say about their community garden.

*"It is fun and a good place to play catchy or hide and seek."*

*"There's lots of beautiful, vibrant flowers and lots of things to play with."*

*"It is a great place for a picnic. It's nice and quiet and peaceful."*

*"It is a great place to spend time with your family."*

1 Stucca, Hillswick
2 Wirligert, Aith
3 Walls
4 Easter Skeld
5 Kalliness, Weisdale
6 Fraser Park, Scalloway
7 Toogs, Burra
8 Bigton Park
9 Baltasound
10 Aywick
11 Symbister
12 Nesting Primary School
13 King George V Park
14 Quoys, Lerwick
15 Gulberwick
16 Cunningsburgh
17 Hoswick play park
18 Sandwick Central
19 Fair Isle Primary School

Sarah Kay's Garden

**DID YOU KNOW?**

The residents of one of Lerwick's lanes have made a fun and interactive community space, next time you are in the lanes see if you can find it.

## Tick if you made it!

- Stucca, Hillswick ○
- Wirligert, Aith ○
- Walls Play Park ○
- Easter Skeld Play Park ○
- Kalliness Play Park ○
- Fraser Park, Scalloway ○
- Toogs Play Park, Burra ○
- Bigton Play Park ○
- Baltasound Play Park ○
- Aywick Play Park ○
- Symbister Play Park ○
- Nesting Primary School ○
- King George V Park ○
- Quoys Play Park ○
- Gulberwick Play Park ○
- Cunningsburgh Play Park ○
- Hoswick Play Park ○
- Sandwick Central Play Park ○
- Fair Isle Primary School ○
- Lea Gardens ○
- Sarah Kay's Garden ○
- North Roe Community Garden ○

# Camping & Caravanning

**Camping Bods:** The Shetland Amenity Trust www.camping-bods.com/ – Phone: 01595 694688
**Breiwick Café and Caravan Park (Wigwams):** Phone: 01806 503345
**Burravoe Wigwams (Brae):** www.facebook.com/BurravoeWigwams – Phone: 01806 522575
**Bridge End Outdoor Centre:** www.bridgeendoutdoors.com – Phone: 01595 859486
**Islesburgh Youth Hostel:** www.shetland.gov.uk/islesburgh/Hostel.asp – Phone: 01595 745100
**Gardiesfauld Youth Hostel:** www.facebook.com/gardiesfauldhostel – Phone: 01957 755279
**Voxter Outdoor Centre:** www.voxteroutdoorcentre.co.uk/

### Camping Böds
1 Betty Mouats - Scatness
2 Nesbister - Whiteness
3 Skeld
4 Voe House - Walls
5 Sail Loft – Voe
6 Grieve House – Whalsay
7 Johnnie Notions – Eshaness
8 Windhouse Lodge – Yell
9 Aithbank – Fetlar

*Camping*

*Johnnie Notions Böd, Eshaness*

*Aithbank Böd, Fetlar*

*Skeld Caravan Park*

*Breakfast at Gardiesfauld Youth Hostel*

*Shana, Kayla-Marie and Bobby having breakfast at the blue wigwam, Eshaness.*

There are lots of great places to explore in Shetland. You can go camping with a tent, tour Shetland with a caravan or stay in a böd or hostel. If you go camping with a tent you should check first with the landowner and remember to use the country code.

You can find caravanning and campsites with hook up points around Shetland. At Braewick and Brae you can stay in wooden wigwams which is a really fun experience.

From April to the end of October you can stay in a camping böd. In Shetland, a Böd was a building used to house fishermen and their gear during the fishing season and the word is now used to describe this basic type of accommodation. Some of the böds have no electricity!

Other fantastic places to stay are the Bridge End Outdoor Centre, Gardiesfauld Youth Hostel in Unst, Voxter Outdoor Centre near Brae and Islesburgh House Hostel in Lerwick.

## CAMPING AND CARAVAN SITES
- Gardisfauld Hostel Caravan and Camp Site
- Burravoe Pier Trust Caravan and Camping Park
- Breiwick Café and Caravan Park, Eshaness
- Delting Boating Club Caravan Park
- South Nesting Caravan Park
- Skeld Caravan and Campsite
- Bridge End Outdoor Centre Caravan and Camping Park
- Aithsvoe Marina Caravan Park, Cunningsburgh
- Levenwick Campsite

Other places have hook up facilities for caravans and campervans such as Bressay Marina, Collafirth Pier and the Ness Boating Club.

### Tick if you have been...
- Camping in a tent ◯
- Camping in a wigwam ◯
- Camping in a böd ◯
- Caravanning ◯
- Bridge End Outdoor Centre ◯
- Gardiesfauld Youth Hostel ◯
- Islesburgh House Hostel ◯
- Voxter Outdoor Centre ◯

# Leisure Centres

*Oliver in the toddlers pool at Clickimin*

*The inflatable at Scalloway pool.*

*The climbing wall at Aith.*

*Zain at the most northerly leisure centre in the UK at Baltasound, Unst.*

*Badminton at Clickimin.*

- Unst Leisure Centre
- Yell Leisure Centre
- North Mainland Leisure Centre
- Whalsay Leisure Centre
- West Mainland Leisure Centre
- Clickimin Leisure Complex
- Scalloway Pool
- South Mainland Pool

**The Shetland Recreational Trust website has information on the activities, timetables and classes provided at all their facilities – www.srt.org.uk**

## DID YOU KNOW?

Before the leisure centres were built children in Shetland learned to swim in the sea. This photograph was taken in 1960 and shows a teacher giving pupils from Scalloway Primary School diving lessons from the Blacksness pier.

Shetland has eight sports centres which are run by the Shetland Recreational Trust. The **Scalloway and South Mainland swimming pools** are fantastic, and both have a bubble pool as well as a toddler's pool and main pool. The other six venues are leisure centres offering a range of other sporting facilities as well as swimming pools.

Unst has the most northerly leisure centre in Britain and has lots to offer including a squash court and a full-sized football pitch. The **West Mainland Leisure Centre** has a great climbing wall and you can book climbing lessons with qualified instructors. **The North Mainland Leisure Centre** has a crazy golf course outside!

All the leisure centres including the ones in **Yell** and **Whalsay** have facilities for indoor sports such as badminton and netball. **Clickimin Leisure Complex** in Lerwick is the biggest sports centre in Shetland. It has a 25m swimming pool and two water slides. Clickimin has many other facilities which include soft play, a running track and a covered football pitch called the **60:40**.

### Tick if you made it!

- Unst Leisure Centre ◯
- Yell Leisure Centre ◯
- Whalsay Leisure Centre ◯
- North Mainland Leisure Centre ◯
- Scalloway Pool ◯
- Clickimin Leisure Complex ◯
- South Mainland Pool ◯
- West Mainland Leisure Centre ◯

# Sports

There are many opportunities for bairns to be active in Shetland. There are clubs and classes in as many different types of sports as you can imagine.

**For more information on sports, email:** sportandleisure@shetland.gov.uk – Phone: 01595 744006

### Active Schools
The Active Schools team in Shetland help to inspire and motivate kids to become more active more often. They work with teachers, schools, club coaches and volunteers to organise afterschool and weekend clubs for kids to come along and try new sports.

### Sport for All
Shetland Sport for All is a voluntary sports hub set up to support people living with a disability to access and enjoy sport and physical activity. The group work to raise awareness of disability sport by supporting local sports clubs while also running some of their own events. If you would like more information on how they could help support you or your family please email them at: shetlandsportforall@yahoo.com

**SHETLAND SPORT FOR ALL** — anyone can - everyone can

**The Shetland Gymnastics Club.**

**SPORTS**
- Football
- Netball
- Badminton
- Squash
- Rugby
- Martial Arts
- Hockey
- Swimming
- Baton Twirling
- Pony Riding
- Sailing
- Tennis
- Archery
- Fencing
- Gymnastics
- Athletics
- Trampolining
- Dancing
- Bowling
- Yoga
- Cycling
- Golf
- Skate Boarding

Peerie Yogis

Sophie Wright enjoying racing on her bike.

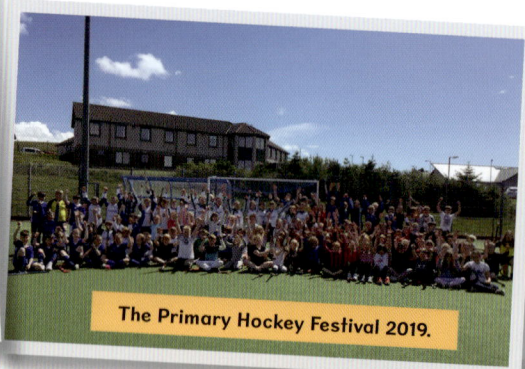

The Primary Hockey Festival 2019.

Football

Baltasound Junior High School, the UK's most northerly school, has achieved a GOLD School Sport Award.

"I love playing rugby with my friends. It is a great sport for anyone. We do running drills and play games. It was amazing to see the famous Calcutta Cup in Shetland."
Olivia MacDonald, age 10.

Erin Millar at the **Shetland Pony Riding School.**

**Generation Pound** at Scalloway Rainbows. A programme that fuses music and movement – kids learn new ways to embrace creativity and rock out.

**The Walls Pool** is run by the community and available for private hire. To book phone 01595 809324.

Lori Duncan at the Breed Show. Lori goes to **Da Filsket Riding Club.**

"I have enjoyed sailing for the past two years. I sail for the **Lerwick Boating Club.** The sailing season is from May to October. Through the summer we get to go to regattas all over Shetland and if you come 1st, 2nd or 3rd you can win prizes like trophies, money and medals. The thing I enjoy most about sailing is being out in the fresh air with my friends."
Alfie Duncan, age 11.

# Groups & Clubs

There are many groups and clubs in Shetland where you can meet friends, have fun and take part in a wide range of activities. Here are a few…

## BAMBEENIES

Bambeenies run weekly classes in Lerwick and Brae providing a wide range of activities for parents and children (0-10 years). You can enjoy taking part in baby massage, yoga, sensory play, messy play, story book massage, dance and movement, sling exercise… and lots more. Bambeenies also run toddler groups, school sessions and birthday parties.

www.bambeenies.co.uk
Jenny Teale 0776 6337991

## JUNIOR YOUTH CLUBS

There are lots of Youth Clubs for children across Shetland. From Baltasound to Bigton you can take part in lots of exciting activities from sports to arts and crafts.

Find out more at:
www.shetland.gov.uk/youth_services/
www.facebook.com/shetlandyouthservices

## BROWNIES AND RAINBOWS

Central contact for Brownies and Rainbows:
girlguiding.org.uk

"We think of others and have fun with our friends." Maisie.
"We do crafts and play with our friends." Ella.
"We do lots of fun stuff and the leaders are fun too." Honey.

## BEAVERS, CUBS AND SCOUTS

**BEAVERS**  **cubs**  **Scouts**

**6-8 years**
Beavers try new things and make friends.

"My favourite thing about Beavers is going camping and sleeping in a tent with my friends."
James

**8-10.5 years**
Cubs master new skills and have adventures.

"At Cubs I learnt to tie knots like my Dad and Uncle Jimmy did when they were peerie."
Callum

**10.5-14 years**
Scouts explore the world and challenge themselves.

"Scouts has helped me make new friends and I feel very smart in my uniform."
Anna

Central contact for Beavers, Cubs and Scouts:
scouts.org.uk

## PRE SCHOOL GROUPS
### TINGWALL TODDLERS

The Shetland Community Directory has information about pre school groups under its 'Young People' heading:
communitydirectory.shetland.gov.uk

## PEERIE EXPLORERS OUTSIDE PLAYGROUP

Peerie Explorers is a free outdoor playgroup for preschool children/toddlers (older children are also welcome), based in Lerwick. Their aim is to be a friendly and welcoming group who help encourage outdoor play no matter what the weather – "There's no such thing as bad weather just the wrong clothes". Parents are welcome to share their tips, ideas and experiences on being outdoors with young children. Most weeks they meet at King Harald Street playpark, although we do often go to other places in Lerwick and sometimes venture further out. Look for the Peerie Explorers group on Facebook.

# The Magic Toolbox

In this book we have learned some things about Shetland's history, community, culture and sports. We have seen that in Shetland there are many opportunities for us all to explore and be creative. We can also learn how to look after our mental health. The Magic Toolbox introduces five tools, which help us recognise and look after our emotions. If your school or club would like to take part in fun Magic Toolbox workshops contact: jane_malcolm@hotmail.com

For further information and resources on mental health contact: www.mindyourhead.org.uk or tel. 01595 745035.

## 1. The Still Stone

I hold my still stone
Gently in my hands
Feeling my breathing
Forgetting all my plans.

This moment is special
Right here, right now
Notice the colours and sounds
This moment is special, WOW!

**Tool trick:** Sometimes our thoughts and feelings are so busy that we miss what is right in front of us. The still stone reminds us to enjoy and notice this moment, right now!

## 2. The Spectacular Spectacles

I put on my spectacular specs
I can see how I feel inside
My feelings are moving
Like sea and the tide.

All my feelings are different
Here are words to describe a few,
Light, whizzing, heavy and bright
Spiky, fluffy and new.

**Tool trick:** The spectacular spectacles help us identify and describe our feelings. Everyone notices their feelings in different ways. Some people notice their feelings in their bodies, other people associate their feelings with smells or sounds. You can invent your own tool to help you notice your feelings.

## 3. The Sorting Box

My sorting box has traffic lights
Green, amber and red
It helps me sort my feelings out
From my toes to my head

Green is for letting it GO
Amber is for WAITING
Red is for STOP
This feeling is not abating

**Tool trick:**
The sorting box helps us to sort out our tricky feelings. We can choose to:

1. Let or feelings GO.
2. We can ask our thoughts and feelings to WAIT until we have time and space to deal with them.
3. If a thought or feeing is very important we can choose to STOP and attend to it now. Sometimes we might need to share our feelings with someone we trust like our parents, carers or a teacher.

## 4. My Magical Mirror

I hold my magical mirror
So I can see my face
I am very special
I am truly ace!

There is only one of me
I will be my best friend
I will love all of me
From beginning to end.

**Tool trick:**
We are all special! Just as we learn to respect others it is good to love and value ourselves. The magical mirror helps you see that you are special simply for being YOU!

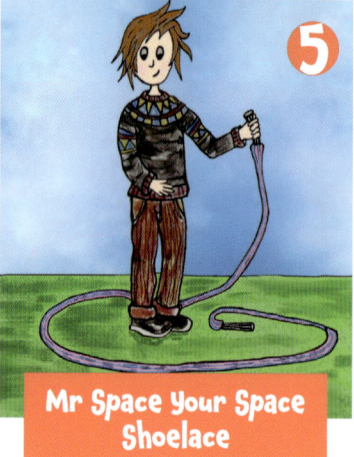

## 5. Mr Space Your Space Shoelace

I draw a line with
My muckle shoelace
It marks out where
I have my space

Sometimes my line stretches far
And sometimes it is near
My line can be any shape
It makes my space clear

I can invite you in my space
Or I can say no
You can invite me into your space
Or you can say 'please go!'

**Tool trick:**
The "my space your space shoelace" helps us to learn about boundaries. We can decide who we share our space with and we can learn to respect other people's space too.

# Your Own Shetland Adventures!

**Use this page to draw, stick photos and write about your very own Shetland Adventures!**

# QUIZ

**Now that you have read the book you can have some fun! See how many questions you can answer in this quiz!**

## QUESTIONS

1. How many sheep are there for every person in Shetland?
2. How high is Shetland's tallest hill?
3. What is felsite and who used it?
4. What was used to make the mortar, which holds the stones together in the Scalloway Castle?
5. What language do 95% of Shetland's place names come from?
6. What unusual item was found with the St Ninian's Isle Treasure?
7. What was the Shetland Bus?
8. What is a boat noost?
9. Why was Johnnie Notions a genius?
10. What did Queen Victoria give Betty Mouat and why?
11. What are some of the differences between a classroom a hundred years ago and today?
12. What was the original capital of Shetland and why did Lerwick become the capital?
13. What type of transport do we not have in Shetland?
14. What do Trows love the sound of?
15. If someone gave you a kokkaloorie and a smoorikin what two things would they be giving you?
16. When was the first Up Helly A' torch lit procession?
17. What is a tushkar?
18. How far does a tirrck fly each year?
19. What is a scaddiemans head?
20. What special thing is found at the Keen of Hamar?
21. Where is the most northerly bus shelter and leisure centre in the UK?
22. What would you need to make a windy craa?
23. Where would you find a hentilaget?

## ANSWERS

1. ..................................................
2. ..................................................
3. ..................................................
4. ..................................................
5. ..................................................
6. ..................................................
7. ..................................................
8. ..................................................
9. ..................................................
10. ..................................................
11. ..................................................
12. ..................................................
13. ..................................................
14. ..................................................
15. ..................................................
16. ..................................................
17. ..................................................
18. ..................................................
19. ..................................................
20. ..................................................
21. ..................................................
22. ..................................................
23. ..................................................

# Bibliography:

**The following books and articles really helped us in putting this book together!**

*A Kist of Emigrants* by J. Laughton Johnston, Published by The Shetland Times Ltd 2010.

*A Photographic Guide to Shetland's History* by David Malcolm, Published by The Shetland Times Ltd 2018.

'*A Vehement thirst after knowledge*' *Four Centuries of Education in Shetland* by John J. Graham, Published by The Shetland Times Ltd 1998.

*Birds of a Shetland Summer* by Visit Shetland, 2007.

*Shetland in Statistics 2017 (No 43),* Published by Economic Development, Shetland Islands Council 2017.

*Shetland Museum and Archives Guidebook,* Shetland Amenity Trust.

The Incoming Project, *Incoming, Some Shetland Voices* edited by Raman Mundair, Published by Shetland Museum and Archives, 2014.

*The Shetland Dictionary* by John J Graham, Published by The Shetland Times Ltd, 1993, revised 1999.

# References:

Cool Creatures page – quotes Paul Harvey (page 12) in *Birds of a Shetland Summer,* Visit Shetland, 2007.

# Websites Frequently referred to:

Shetland.org website: ***www.shetland.org***

Shetland Museum and Archives website: ***www.shetlandmuseumandarchives.org.uk***

Shetland ForWirds: ***www.shetlanddialect.org.uk***

# Photo credits:

### Introduction
60 North by Laurie Goodlad
Puffin Trail in Unst by Agnes Szobonya-Dombovari
David in Museum Store by Jane Cockayne
Cake Fridge by Jane Cockayne
Bus Shelter by Saro Saravanan
Ronas Hill by Alex Purbrick
Merrie Dancers by Lynn McCormack
Sullom Voe by Alex Purbrick

### Ancient History
Staneydale 1 by Laurie Goodlad
Staneydale 2 by Laurie Goodlad
Jarlshof Hansi by Laurie Goodlad
Jarlshof Aerial from Shetland Museum & Archives
Mousa Broch by Laurie Goodlad
Storm Petrel by Hugh Harrop
Felsite Axe by Laurie Goodlad
Painted Pebbles by Laurie Goodlad

### Old Scatness Broch & Iron Age Village
Spot the Difference 1 by Jane Cockayne
Spot the Difference 2 by Bryan Mouat
Chris Dyer Guiding by Jane Cockayne
Old Scatness Aerial Photo by Val Turner, Shetland Amenity Trust
Bear Stone by Jane Cockayne

### The Vikings and Stewart Earls
Longship & House Replica by David Malcolm
Girlsta Loch by Catherine Corbett
Viking Oven by Catherine Corbett
Catpund Quarry by Catherine Corbett
Scalloway Castle by Jane Cockayne
Norse Place Name by Jane Cockayne

### Houses and Homes
Croft House Museum by Laurie Goodlad
Thatching at Easthouse, Burra by Laurie Goodlad
Agricultural Tools from the Past by Laurie Goodlad
Spinning by Fireside from Shetland Museum & Archives
Tove and Heating Pipes by Floortje Robertson Matthew
Tove and her New House by Floortje Robertson Matthew
Supermarket by Jane Cockayne

### Crofts Today
Burland Croft 1 by Jane Cockayne
Burland Croft 2 by Jane Cockayne
Burland Croft 3 by Jane Cockayne
The Outpost Flag by David Malcolm
The Outpost Goat by Mary Boyd
The Outpost Emu by Jane Cockayne
The Outpost Pigs by Jane Cockayne
The Outpost Wallaby by David Malcolm
Garths Croft by Floortje Robertson Matthew
Garths Croft 2 by Floortje Robertson Matthew

### The Shetland Bus
Sub Chaser KNM *Vigra* by Ria Moncrieff
Norway House by Ria Moncrieff
Shetland Bus Memorial 1 (with Johanny) by Ria Moncrieff
Shetland Bus Memorial 2 by Jane Cockayne

### St Ninian's Isle Treasure
St Ninian's Chapel Site by Saro Saravanan
St Ninian's Beach by Saro Saravanan
St Ninian's Treasure from National Museums Scotland
St Ninian's Story by Jane Cockayne & Laurie Goodlad
Douglas Coutts by Thomas Cockayne

### Past and Present
Toys Past from Shetland Museum & Archives
Toys Present by Jane Cockayne
Windy Craa by Jane Cockayne
Butter Past (Bog Butter) by Jenny Murray
Butter Present by Jane Cockayne
Camera Past by Jane Cockayne
Camera Present by Jane Cockayne
Baby Bottle Past by Jane Cockayne
Baby Bottle Present by Cândida Jardim
Rivlins from Shetland Museum & Archives
Marnie's Shoes by Rachel Jamieson
Boat Noost from Shetland Museum & Archives
Car Park by Jane Cockayne

### Curious Characters
Barbara Pitcairn by Bryan Mouat
Betty Mouat by Bryan Mouat
Gunnister Man by Bryan Mouat
Hazel Tindall by Bryan Mouat
Jim O' Berry by Bryan Mouat
Johnnie Notions by Bryan Mouat
Mary the Eagle Bairn by Bryan Mouat

### School
Slates by Jane Cockayne
Hamnavoe Classroom 1912 from Shetland Museum and Archives
Hamnavoe Classroom Present by Jane Cockayne
Fetlar – photo of Darcy by Claire Cook
Darcy's Drawing by Darcy Cook
Home Education 1 by Ali Laver
Home Education 2 by Ali Laver

### Fishing and The Sea
Sixareen from Shetland Museum & Archives
Pelagic Boat, *Serene* by Jane Cockayne
The *Swan* under sail by The Swan Trust
The *Swan* & Happy Hansel School, 2019 by Jane Cockayne
Hansi in Grandad's Boat by Laurie Goodlad
Fish Market by Laurie Goodlad
Oscar Charlie and Life Boat by Laurie Goodlad
Aff in Geordie's Boat by Catherine Corbett
Sumburgh Lighthouse 1 by Saro Saravanan
Sumburgh Lighthouse 2 by Saro Saravanan
At da mussel lines by Shyrleen Pottinger
Wooton Lass by Ability Shetland

### Transport
Earl of Zetland from Shetland Museum & Archives
Whalsay Ferry by Jane Cockayne
Inter Island Flight by Rory Tallack
Northlink Drive on by Debbie Morgan
Northlink Cabin by Debbie Morgan
Sumburgh Plane by Jane Cockayne
Joe with Car by Ian Simpson
Artwork 1 by Arulaa, Kashi and Bodhi Mundair
Artwork 2 by Arulaa, Kashi and Bodhi Mundair

### Coming and Going
Dr De Sylva from Shetland Museum & Archives
Magnus and Torafn Leask by Nicki Leask
Prasheeta by Saro Saravanan
Sasha by Maria Shlyannikova
Artwork 1 by Arulaa, Kashi and Bodhi Mundair
Artwork 2 by Arulaa, Kashi and Bodhi Mundair

### Museums
Oliver In Shetland Museum by Mary Boyd
Quendale Mill by Jane Cockayne
The Croft House Museum Exterior by Jane Cockayne
The Croft House Museum Interior by Ria Moncrieff
Tangwick Ha by Jane Cockayne
Wedding Dress at Tangwick Ha by Jane Cockayne
Whalsay Heritage Centre by Jane Cockayne
Scalloway Museum by Jane Cockayne

### Dialect
GillyB Papercut by Gilly Bridle

### Folklore
Folklore Characters by Joahnny & Raffi Bruce
Road Sign by Jane Cockayne
Feilnadringa Boys by Debbie Morgan

### Arts and Entertainment
Creativity Club Felting Group by Jane Cockayne
Creativity Club Felting Individual by Jane Cockayne
Shetland Community School of Ballet provided by Matthew Lawrence
Inferno provided by Jennifer Teale
Cinema by Jane Cockayne
Shana practicing piano by Shyrleen Pottinger
Library 1 Chloe Tallack
Library 2 Chloe Tallack
Shetland Bairns Open Exhibition 2019 from Shetland Arts
Shetland Community Orchestra by Sioban Tekcan
Aa Fired Up by Aa Fired Up
3 Fiddlers by Shyrleen Pottinger
Mareel Time Capsule by Jane Cockayne

### Song
Louie Coyne sings Peerie Lavericks by Jane Cockayne
Laverick/Skylark photo by Hugh Harrop

### Festivals & Shows
Peerie Spang by Louise Johnson
Torch lit procession by Kevin Osborn
Day procession by Kevin Osborn
Adam at Carnival by Brydon Leslie
2015 SMUHA Lesley Simpson by Kevin Osborn
505 Show by Debbie Morgan

Tractor Show by June Cockayne
Wedding procession by Ben Mullay

### Knitting
Knitting while carrying peats from Shetland Museum & Archives
Triple Tone Circular Scarf by Terri Malcomson
Shetland Peerie Makkers logo by Tracey Hawkins
Shetland Peerie Makkers 1 by Tracey Hawkins
Shetland Peerie Makkers 2 by Tracey Hawkins
The Journey of Wool step 1 by June Brown; Steps 2-5 by Jamiesons of Shetland; Step 6 by Tracey Hawkins
Fair Isle Burra Bear by Wendy Inkster

### Scones and Bannocks
Hani 1 by Meriem Nicolson
Hani 2 by Meriem Nicolson
Eva by Leona Cluness
Bannocks by Nicola Johnson

### Cari's Peat
Put da faels doon by Jacqueline Laurenson
Casting paets by Jacqueline Laurenson
Paets in a dyk by Jacqueline Laurenson
Clear da gref o' clods by Jacqueline Laurenson
Raising paets by Jacqueline Laurenson
Bag da paets & take dem hame by Jacqueline Laurenson
Cari's paet bank bridge! by Jacqueline Laurenson
Viking Glove by Jenny Murray
Bog Butter by Jenny Murray
Gunnister Man by Bryan Mouat
Paet Fire by Jane Cockayne

### Fun things to do Outside
Smugglers Cave Rope Ladder by Jane Cockayne
Smugglers Cave Interior by Jane Cockayne
Freddie Fishing, Burn of Lunklet by Emma Waterhouse
Adam and David on Path by Jane Cockayne
Steens of Stofast Climbing by Jane Cockayne
Steens of Stofast 3 Bairns by Jane Cockayne
Ability Shetland All Terrain Wheelchair 1 from Ability Shetland
Ability Shetland All Terrain Wheelchair 2 from Ability Shetland

### Beaches
Minn 1, Burra by Jane Cockayne
Minn 2, Burra by Jane Cockayne
Tresta, Fetlar by Jane Cockayne
Norwick, Unst by Jane Cockayne
St Ninians Zak from Ability Shetland
St Ninians Group by Jane Cockayne
St Ninians Surf Boards by Jane Cockayne
Sand Mandala by Alex Purbrick

### Aboot Da Banks
Rockpool with Bairns 1 by Jonathan Kerr
Rockpool with Bairns 2 by Jonathan Kerr
Bare Feet & Seaweed by Jonathan Kerr
Shells by Jonathan Kerr
Crab in Hand by Jonathan Kerr
Crab in Hand 2 by Jonathan Kerr
Pink Bucket by Jonathan Kerr
Grottie Buckies by Laurie Goodlad

### Woodlands
Da Gairdins by Jonathan Kerr
Kergord Rope Swing by Jane Cockayne
Michael's Wood Dinosaur by Tracey Millar
Michael's Wood Harrison from Ability Shetland
Voxter by Jane Cockayne
Shetland Amenity Trust Key Highlights 2019 from Shetland Amenity Trust

### Arts & Crafts with Natural Minerals
Memory Stick 1 by Alex Purbrick
Memory Stick 2 by Alex Purbrick
Memory Stick 3 by Alex Purbrick
Memory Stick 4 by Alex Purbrick
Mud Picture 1 by Alex Purbrick
Mud Picture 2 by Alex Purbrick
Mud Picture 3 by Alex Purbrick
Mud Picture 4 by Alex Purbrick
Beach Art Man by Jane Cockayne
Shell Sculpture by Jane Cockayne Creativity Club
Felt Pictures by Jane Cockayne Creativity Club
Emma's Felting Fun by Jane Cockayne Creativity Club
Alisha Stone Painting by Jane Cockayne
Painted Stones by Jane Cockayne
Woolly Character by Jane Cockayne

### Cool Creatures
Orca by Hugh Harrop
Tirrick by Hugh Harrop
Otter by Hugh Harrop
Shetland Bumble Bee by Hugh Harrop
Puffin by Saro Saravanan
Shetland Pony by Jane Cockayne
Hillswick Wildlife Sanctuary Dratsie by Jan & Pete Bevington
RSPB logo from Karen MacKelvie
Shetland Nature Festival logo from Rory Tallack, Shetland Amenity Trust

### Geopark
Eshaness by Rory Tallack
Shingly Geo by Rory Tallack
Fossil Fish by Rory Tallack
Keen of Hamar by Billy Fox
Edmonston's Chickweed by Wendy Dickson
Thea Exploring Quarff by Rory Tallack

### Looking after the Environment
Woodwick Beach Redd Up from Shetland Amenity Trust
Shetland farm Dairies by Jane Cockayne
Da Voar Redd Up 2019 statistics from Shetland Amenity Trust

### Parks and Community Gardens
Oliver King, George V Park, Lerwick by Jane Cockayne
Zain, Whalsay Leisure Centre Park by Jane Cockayne
Rocco & Jones, Nesting Primary School by Dhanika Drakeford
Jones at Sandwick School by Dhanika Drakeford
David on Zip Wire by Jane Cockayne
Park Lane Community Garden by Laurie Goodlad
Hoswick Play Park by Hannah McNicol
Nesting Primary School by Hannah McNicol
North Roe Community Garden 1 by North Roe School
North Roe Community Garden 2 by North Roe School
David, Walls Park by Jane Cockayne
Sarah Kay's Garden by Sarah Kay
Hoswick Cake Cupboard by Carrie MacDonald

### Camping and Caravanning
Chloe and Phoebe in tent by Jonathan Kerr
Group of Bairns with Backpack by Jonathan Kerr
Boy and 2 tents by Jonathan Kerr
Johnnie Notions Böd by Laurie Goodlad
Aithbank Böd by Laurie Goodlad
Caravan Interior by Saro Saravanan
Caravan Exterior by Saro Saravanan
Eshaness Wigwams by Shyrleen Pottinger
David and Tom Gardiesfauld by Jane Cockayne

### Leisure Centre
Oliver, Clickimin Toddlers Pool by Jane Cockayne
Climbing Wall by Jane Cockayne
Badminton by Jane Cockayne
Unst Leisure Centre by Jane Cockayne
Inflatable Scalloway Pool by Jane Cockayne
Blacksness Pier from Shetland Museum & Archives

### Sport
Shetland Pony Riding School – Erin by Laura Matthieson
Da Filskit Riding Club – Lori by Donna Murray
Shetland Gymnastics Club provided by Shetland Gymnastics Club, Julie Grant
David Football by Jane Cockayne
Freddie Football by Emma Waterhouse
Walls Pool by Jane Cockayne
Sport for All logo from Donna Murray
Sophie racing on bike by Donna Murray
The Primary Hockey Festival provided by Jennifer Thomson, Active Schools
Sailing – Alfie by Donna Murray
Shetland Junior Rugby by Carrie MacDonald
Generation Pound by Carrie MacDonald
Peerie Yogis by Donna Mainland

### Groups and Clubs
Brownies 1 by Cyndi Pottinger
Rainbows by Cyndi Pottinger
Peerie Explorers by Rachel Williamson
Junior Youth Clubs 1 by Martin Summers
Junior Youth Clubs 2 by Martin Summers
Bambeenies 1 by Jennifer Teale
Bambeenies 2 by Jennifer Teale
Tingwall Toddlers by Mary Boyd
Beavers logo from Cathy Mann
Cubs logo from Cathy Mann
Scouts logo from Cathy Mann

### The Magic Toolbox
The Magic Toolbox, Scalloway by Jane Cockayne
Tool 1 The Still Stone by Jane Cockayne
Tool 2 The Spectacular Spectacles by Jane Cockayne
Tool 3 The Sorting Box by Jane Cockayne
Tool 4 My Magical Mirror by Jane Cockayne
Tool 5 My Space Your Space Shoelace by Jane Cockayne

### Front Cover
All the photos on the front cover are in the book apart from 'Girl with Sheep' which was taken by Chloe Tallack

### Back Cover
David outside the *Shetland Times* by Jane Cockayne